CHRISTIAN MARRIAGE

CHRISTIAN MARRIAGE

The Worship of God

Supplemental Liturgical Resource 3

Prepared by

The Office of Worship
for the
Presbyterian Church (U.S.A.)
and the
Cumberland Presbyterian Church

Published by
The Westminster Press
Philadelphia

For acknowledgments, see pages 119–120.

Published by The Westminster Press®
Philadelphia, Pennsylvania

PRINTED IN THE UNITED STATES OF AMERICA
2 4 6 8 9 7 5 3

Library of Congress Cataloging-in-Publication Data

Presbyterian Church (U.S.A.)
   Christian marriage.

   (Supplemental liturgical resource ; 3)
   Bibliography: p.
   1. Marriage service—Liturgy—Texts. 2. Presbyterian Church (U.S.A.)—Liturgy—Texts. 3. Cumberland Presbyterian Church—Liturgy—Texts. 4. Presbyterian Church—United States——Liturgy—Texts. I. Office of Worship for the Presbyterian Church (U.S.A.) and the Cumberland Presbyterian Church. II. Title. III. Series: Presbyterian Church (U.S.A.). Supplemental liturgical resource ; 3.
BX8969.5.P74 1986   264'.05137   85-29571
ISBN 0-664-24033-X (pbk.)

CONTENTS

PREFACE

In 1980, the antecedent denominations of the Presbyterian Church (U.S.A.) took action to begin the process to develop "a new book of services for corporate worship, including a Psalter, hymns, and other worship aids." The churches asked that over the "next several years a variety of worship resources be made available . . . for trial use throughout the church before any publication is finalized." In this action the church expressed a hope that such a book and the process leading to it "would provide a new instrument for the renewal of the church at its life-giving center." Subsequent action by the Cumberland Presbyterian Church made it a partner in the project.

Christian Marriage is the third volume in the series of trial-use liturgical resources that is resulting from the General Assembly actions. Previous volumes include: *The Service for the Lord's Day* (Supplemental Liturgical Resource 1), and *Holy Baptism and Services for the Renewal of Baptism* (Supplemental Liturgical Resource 2). In addition, *The Funeral: A Service of Witness to the Resurrection* (Supplemental Liturgical Resource 4) is appearing simultaneously with this volume. Other resources being developed include daily prayer, the psalms, the Christian year, ordination, ministry to the sick and dying, the lectionary, and service music. When the series of resources is completed, the material that will have appeared will be further revised and combined in a new book of services.

In the development of the resources, guidance on worship policy is given by the Advisory Council on Discipleship and Worship through its Committee on Worship.

A task force of persons with expertise in the particular subject of the resource to be developed is appointed by the Administrative Committee of the Office of Worship to prepare a manuscript on an assigned portion of the church's liturgy. In the fall of 1982, a task force was appointed to prepare the wedding liturgy. *Christian Marriage* is the result of the work of that task force.

Those who served on the task force that prepared *Christian Marriage* were Thomas G. Long, chairperson; Betty Peek; Martha Blunt; Thomas E. Pass; Craig D. Erickson, consultant; and Harold M. Daniels, staff.

Each manuscript that is developed in the Supplemental Liturgical Resource series is carefully reviewed by the Worship Committee of the Advisory Council on Discipleship and Worship, which makes suggestions for its revision. Members of the Worship Committee reviewing *Christian Marriage* were J. Barrie Shepherd, chairperson; Moffett Swaim Churn; Jay Dee Conrad; Melva W. Costen; Frances M. Gray; Irene Overton; Franklin E. Perkins; Donald W. Stake; Helen Wright; James G. Kirk, staff; Elizabeth J. Villegas, staff; and Harold M. Daniels, adjunct staff.

Christian Marriage was extensively field-tested. Suggestions were also sought from liturgical scholars both in the Reformed and in other traditions. The evaluations and suggestions that were received contributed greatly to the improvement of this resource, and we are therefore indebted to many people for their invaluable assistance.

Responding to the field-testing and review, the task force prepared the final draft of this resource and presented it to the Administrative Committee of the Office of Worship. The Administrative Committee, which has overseen the work of the task force during the years the resource was being developed, then approved the manuscript for publication. Those who served on the Administrative Committee during the time *Christian Marriage* was being developed were Melva W. Costen; Lucile L. Hair (former chairperson); Helen Hamilton; Collier S. Harvey; James G. Kirk; Wynn McGregor; Ray Meester; Robert D. Miller; David C. Partington (current chairperson); Dorothea Snyder (former chairperson); Robert Stigall; Darius L. Swann; James Vande Berg; Harold M. Daniels, staff; and Marion L. Liebert, staff.

We invite your evaluation of this resource presented to the church for trial use as it anticipates a new book of services. Send your comments to the Office of Worship, 1044 Alta Vista Road, Louisville, Kentucky 40205.

HAROLD M. DANIELS, Director
Office of Worship

AN ORDER FOR CHRISTIAN MARRIAGE

OUTLINE OF
CHRISTIAN MARRIAGE: RITE I
A Service for General Use

Entrance
Sentences of Scripture
Statement on the Gift of Marriage
Prayer
Declarations of Intent
Affirmations of the Families
Affirmation of the Congregation
(Psalm, Hymn, or Spiritual)
Scripture and Sermon
(Psalm, Hymn, or Spiritual)
Vows
Exchange of Rings (or Other Symbols)
Prayer (and Lord's Prayer)
Announcement of Marriage
Charge to the Couple
Benediction
(Psalm, Hymn, Spiritual, or Anthem)

CHRISTIAN MARRIAGE: RITE I
A Service for General Use

ENTRANCE

*gather, music appropriate to the praise of God may be
appointed time the bride, groom, and other members
party present themselves and stand before the minister.
ay stand with the couple. A psalm, hymn, spiritual,
be sung, or instrumental music may be played, as the
enters.*

SENTENCES OF SCRIPTURE

*Either before or after the entrance, the people are called to worship
with these or other words from Scripture:*

God is love, and those who abide in love
abide in God, and God abides in them.   *1 John 4:16*

Or

This is the day the Lord has made.
Let us rejoice and be glad in it.   *Psalm 118:24*

STATEMENT ON THE GIFT OF MARRIAGE

The minister shall say:

We have gathered in the presence of God
to give thanks for the gift of marriage,
to witness the joining together of _____ and _____,
to surround them with our prayers,
and to ask God's blessing upon them,
so that they may be strengthened for their life together
and nurtured in their love for God.

God created us male and female,
and gave us marriage
so that husband and wife may help and comfort each other,
living faithfully together in plenty and in want,
in joy and in sorrow,

in sickness and in health,
throughout all their days.

God gave us marriage
for the full expression of the love between a man and a woman.
In marriage a woman and a man belong to each other,
and with affection and tenderness
freely give themselves to each other.

God gave us marriage
for the well-being of human society,
for the ordering of family life,
and for the birth and nurture of children.

God gave us marriage as a holy mystery
in which a man and a woman are joined together,
and become one,
just as Christ is one with the church.

In marriage, husband and wife are called to a new way of life,
created, ordered, and blessed by God.
This way of life must not be entered into carelessly,
or from selfish motives,
but responsibly, and prayerfully.

We rejoice that marriage is given by God,
blessed by our Lord Jesus Christ,
and sustained by the Holy Spirit.
Therefore, let marriage be held in honor among all.

PRAYER

The minister says:

Let us pray:

Gracious God, you are always faithful in your love for us.
Look mercifully upon _____ and _____,
who have come seeking your blessing.
Let your Holy Spirit rest upon them
so that with steadfast love
they may honor the promises they make this day,
through Jesus Christ our Savior.

Amen.

DECLARATIONS OF INTENT

The minister addresses the bride and groom individually:

_____, having heard how God has created, ordered, and blessed
   the covenant of marriage,
do you affirm your desire and intention
to enter this covenant?

   Answer:

I do.

   Or, if both are baptized, the following may be used.

_____, in your baptism
you have been called to union with Christ and the church.
Do you intend to honor this calling
through the covenant of marriage?

   Answer:

I do.

AFFIRMATIONS OF THE FAMILIES

The minister may address the families of the bride and groom:

(Names of family members) _____,
do you give your blessing to _____ and _____,
and promise to do everything in your power to uphold them in their
   marriage?

   Answer:

omit

Or

We (I) give our (my) blessing   **We (I) do.**
and promise our (my) loving
  support.

The families may be seated.

AFFIRMATION OF THE CONGREGATION

The minister may then address the congregation. The congregation may stand.

Will all of you witnessing these vows
do everything in your power to uphold _____ and _____ in their
  marriage?

Answer:

We will.

A psalm, hymn, spiritual, or anthem may be sung.

SCRIPTURE AND SERMON

The following, or a similar prayer for illumination, may be said.

God of mercy,
you have never broken your covenant with us,
and you free us to live together
in the power of your faithful love.
Amid all the changing words of our generation,
may we hear your eternal Word that does not change.
Then may we respond to your gracious promises
with faithful and obedient lives;
through our Lord Jesus Christ.

Amen.

Scripture shall be read.

A brief sermon may follow.

A psalm, hymn, spiritual, or other music may be used.

VOWS

The minister addresses the couple:

_____ and _____,
since it is your intention to marry,
join your right hands,
and with your promises
bind yourselves to each other as husband and wife.

> *The bride and groom face each other and join right hands. Then, they shall say their vows to each other, in turn.*

Or

The man says:

I, _____, take you, _____,
   to be my wife;
and I promise,
before God and these
   witnesses,
to be your loving and faithful
   husband;
in plenty and in want;
in joy and in sorrow;
in sickness and in health;
as long as we both shall live.

The man says:

Before God and these
   witnesses,
I, _____, take you, _____,
   to be my wife,
and I promise to love you,
and to be faithful to you
as long as we both shall live.

The woman says:

I, _____ , take you, _____ ,
   to be my husband;
and I promise,
before God and these
   witnesses,
to be your loving and faithful
   wife;
in plenty and in want;
in joy and in sorrow;
in sickness and in health;
as long as we both shall live.

The woman says:

Before God and these
   witnesses,
I, _____ , take you, _____ ,
   to be my husband,
and I promise to love you,
and to be faithful to you,
as long as we both shall live.

EXCHANGE OF RINGS (OR OTHER SYMBOLS)

If rings are to be exchanged, the minister says to the couple:

What do you bring as the sign of your promise?

When the rings are presented the minister may say the following prayer.

By your blessing, O God,
may these rings be to _____ and _____
symbols of unending love and faithfulness,
reminding them of the covenant they have made this day,
through Jesus Christ our Lord.

Amen.

The bride and groom shall exchange rings using these or other appro-
priate words.

Or

The one giving the ring
says:

      , I give you this ring
as a sign of our covenant,
in the name of the Father,
and of the Son,
and of the Holy Spirit.

As each ring is given, the
one giving the ring says:

This ring I give you,
as a sign of our constant faith
and abiding love,
in the name of the Father,
and of the Son,
and of the Holy Spirit.

The one receiving the ring
says:

I receive this ring
as a sign of our covenant
in the name of the Father,
and of the Son,
and of the Holy Spirit.

PRAYER

The couple may kneel.

One of the following prayers, or a similar prayer, is said:

Let us pray:

Eternal God,
creator and preserver of all life,
author of salvation
and giver of all grace:
look with favor upon the world you have made and redeemed,
and especially upon   and   .

Give them wisdom and devotion in their common life,
that each may be to the other
a strength in need,
a comfort in sorrow,

a counselor in perplexity,
and a companion in joy.

Grant that their wills may be so knit together in your will,
and their spirits in your Spirit,
that they may grow in love and peace
with you and each other
all the days of their life.

Give them the courage,
when they hurt each other,
to recognize and confess their fault,
and the grace to seek your forgiveness,
and to forgive each other.

Make their life together
a sign of Christ's love to this sinful and broken world,
that unity may overcome estrangement,
forgiveness heal guilt,
and joy conquer despair.

Give them such fulfillment of their mutual love
that they may reach out in concern for others.

[Give to them, if it is your will,
the gift of children,
and the wisdom to bring them up
to know you, to love you,
and to serve you.]

Grant that all who have witnessed these vows today
may find their lives strengthened,
and that all who are married
may depart with their own promises renewed.

Enrich with your grace
all husbands and wives, parents and children,
that, loving and supporting one another,
they may serve those in need
and be a sign of your kingdom.

Grant that the bonds of our common humanity,
by which all your children are united one to another,
may be so transformed by your Spirit
that your peace and justice may fill the earth,
through Jesus Christ our Lord.

Amen.

> *Or*

Eternal God,
without your grace no promise is sure.
Strengthen _____ and _____ with patience, kindness, gentleness,
and all other gifts of your Spirit,
so that they may fulfill the vows they have made.
Keep them faithful to each other and to you.
Fill them with such love and joy
that they may build a home of peace and welcome.
Guide them by your word
to serve you all their days.

Enable us all, O God,
in each of our homes and lives to do your will.
Enrich us with your grace
so that, encouraging and supporting one another,
we may serve those in need
and hasten the coming of peace, love, and justice on earth,
through Jesus Christ our Lord.

Amen.

The Lord's Prayer may be said or sung.

Our Father in heaven,
   hallowed be your name,
   your kingdom come,
   your will be done,
     on earth as in heaven.
Give us today our daily bread.
Forgive us our sins
   as we forgive those
   who sin against us.
Save us from the time of trial
   and deliver us from evil.
For the kingdom, the power,
   and the glory are yours,
now and forever. Amen.

Our Father, who art in heaven,
   hallowed be thy name,
   thy kingdom come,
   thy will be done,
     on earth as it is in heaven.
Give us this day our daily bread;
and forgive us our debts,
   as we forgive our debtors;
and lead us not into temptation,
   but deliver us from evil.
For thine is the kingdom,
   and the power, and the glory,
   forever. Amen.

ANNOUNCEMENT OF MARRIAGE

The minister addresses the congregation:

Before God
and in the presence of this congregation,
_____ and _____ have made their solemn vows to each other.
They have confirmed their promises by the joining of hands
[and by the giving and receiving of rings].
Therefore, I proclaim that they are now husband and wife.

Blessed be the Father and the Son and the Holy Spirit now and
   forever.

The minister joins the couple's right hands.

The congregation may join the minister saying:

Those whom God has joined together
let no one separate.

CHARGE TO THE COUPLE

The minister addresses the couple:

As God's own,
clothe yourselves with compassion,
kindness, and patience,
forgiving each other
as the Lord has forgiven you,
and crown all these things with love,
which binds everything together in perfect harmony.　　*Col. 3:12–14*

Or

Whatever you do, in word or deed,
do everything in the name of the Lord Jesus,
giving thanks to God through him.　　　　　　　　*Col. 3:17*

BENEDICTION

The minister addresses the couple and the congregation:

The Lord bless you and keep you.
The Lord be kind and gracious to you.
The Lord look upon you with favor
and give you peace.　　　　　　　　　　　　*Num. 6:24–26*

Amen.

Or

The grace of Christ attend you,
the love of God surround you,
the Holy Spirit keep you,
that you may live in faith,
abound in hope,
and grow in love,
both now and forevermore.

Amen.

A psalm, hymn, spiritual, or anthem may be sung, or instrumental music may be played as the wedding party leaves.

OUTLINE OF
CHRISTIAN MARRIAGE: RITE II
A Service Based Upon the Service for the Lord's Day

ASSEMBLE IN GOD'S NAME

Gathering of the People
Call to Worship
Psalm, Hymn of Praise, or Spiritual
Confession and Pardon
Act of Praise

PROCLAIM GOD'S WORD

Prayer for Illumination
Lessons from Scripture
Sermon
Creed
Psalm, Hymn, or Spiritual
Christian Marriage
  Statement on the Gift of Marriage
  Prayer
  Declarations of Intent
  Affirmations of the Families
  Affirmation of the Congregation
  (Psalm, Hymn, or Spiritual)
  Vows
  Exchange of Rings (or Other Symbols)
  Prayer (and Lord's Prayer)
  Announcement of Marriage
  Charge to the Couple
  Blessing of the Couple

(Psalm, Hymn, Spiritual, or Anthem)
Prayers of Intercession (Lord's Prayer)

GIVE THANKS TO GOD
——————— *Or* ———————

Preparation of the Table   Prayer of Thanksgiving
Great Prayer of Thanksgiving,   (followed by the Lord's Prayer)
   followed by the Lord's Prayer
Breaking of the Bread
Communion of the People

GO IN GOD'S NAME
Prayer
Psalm, Hymn of Praise, or Spiritual
Charge
Benediction

CHRISTIAN MARRIAGE: RITE II
A Service Based Upon the Service for the Lord's Day

This rite is ordered after the Service for the Lord's Day and is designed for use when the marriage is to be included as a part of the Lord's Day worship or on any other occasion when the full pattern of Christian worship is appropriate. The rite is arranged to allow for the inclusion of the Lord's Supper, if desired.

ASSEMBLE IN GOD'S NAME

GATHERING OF THE PEOPLE

The bride, groom, their families, and other members of the wedding party may gather for worship with the other members of the congregation, or they may enter together before the call to worship. Music may be offered appropriate to the season, to the Scriptural texts of the day, or to the celebration of marriage.

CALL TO WORSHIP

The people shall be called to worship with these, or similar, words:

The Lord be with you.

And also with you.   *Ruth 2:4*

And one of the following:

This is the day the Lord has made;

Let us rejoice and be glad in it.   *Ps. 118:24*

Or

God is love, and those who abide in love abide in God,

And God abides in them.   *1 John 4:16*

Or

Beloved, let us love one another, for love is of God.
All who love are born of God and know God.

All who do not love do not know God,
for God is love.   *1 John 4:7–8*

Psalm, Hymn of Praise, or Spiritual

The people respond to the promises of God by singing praise in a psalm, hymn, or spiritual.

Confession and Pardon

The people are called to confession with these or other sentences of Scripture that promise God's forgiveness:

This is the covenant
which I will make with the house of Israel,
says the Lord:
I will put my law within them,
and I will write it upon their hearts;
and I will be their God,
and they shall be my people.
I will forgive their evil deeds,
and I will remember their sin no more.   *Jer. 31:33–34*

In penitence and faith,
let us confess our sins to almighty God.

The people confess their sins, using this, or a similar, prayer:

**Merciful God,
we confess that we have sinned against you
in thought, word, and deed.
We have not loved you
with our whole heart and mind and strength;
we have not loved our neighbors as ourselves.
In your mercy forgive what we have been,
help us amend what we are,
and direct what we shall be,
so that we may delight in your will
and walk in your ways,
to the glory of your holy name.**

Amen.

Or

Almighty God,
you created us for life together,
but we have turned from your will.
We have not loved as you commanded.
We have broken the promises we have made to you
and to one another.
We have taken much and given little.
Forgive our disobedience, O God,
and strengthen us in love,
so that we may serve you as a faithful people,
and live together in your joy;
through Jesus Christ our Lord.

Amen.

The following may be sung or said:

Lord, have mercy.
Christ, have mercy.
Lord, have mercy.

Assurance of God's forgiving grace is declared by the minister. These
or other words of Scripture may be used:

Hear the good news!

Who is in a position to condemn?
Only Christ,
and Christ died for us,
Christ rose for us,
Christ reigns in power for us,
Christ prays for us.   *Rom. 8:34*

Anyone who is in Christ is a new creation.
The old life has gone:
a new life has begun.   *2 Cor. 5:17*

Friends, believe the gospel.

In Jesus Christ, we are forgiven.

ACT OF PRAISE

A joyful response is sung or said. The people may exchange THE PEACE by offering one another signs of reconciliation.

PROCLAIM GOD'S WORD

PRAYER FOR ILLUMINATION

The following, or a similar prayer for illumination, may be said:

God of mercy,
you have never broken your covenant with us,
and you free us to live together
in the power of your faithful love.
Amid all the changing words of our generation,
may we hear your eternal Word that does not change.
Then may we respond to your gracious promises
with faithful and obedient lives;
through our Lord Jesus Christ.
Amen.

LESSONS FROM SCRIPTURE

Lessons suggested in a lectionary, or other appropriate lessons from both Testaments, shall be read. Between the lessons, the psalm for the day, hymns, spirituals, or anthems related to the lessons may be sung.

SERMON

One or more of the lessons from Scripture is proclaimed in a sermon. An ASCRIPTION OF PRAISE may conclude the sermon.

CREED

The people may say or sing a creed of the church or an affirmation of faith drawn from Scripture.

PSALM, HYMN, OR SPIRITUAL

A psalm, hymn, or spiritual may be sung. The bride, groom, and other members of the wedding party present themselves at this time and stand before the minister. The families may stand with the couple.

CHRISTIAN MARRIAGE

STATEMENT ON THE GIFT OF MARRIAGE

The minister shall say:

_____ and _____ have come to make their marriage vows
in the presence of God
and of this congregation.
Let us now witness their promises to each other
and surround them with our prayers,
giving thanks to God for the gift of marriage
and asking God's blessing upon them,
so that they may be strengthened for their life together
and nurtured in their love for God.

God created us male and female,
and gave us marriage
so that husband and wife may help and comfort each other,
living faithfully together in plenty and in want,
in joy and in sorrow,
in sickness and in health,
throughout all their days.

God gave us marriage
for the full expression of the love between a man and a woman.
In marriage a woman and a man belong to each other,
and with affection and tenderness
freely give themselves to each other.

God gave us marriage
for the well-being of human society,
for the ordering of family life,
and for the birth and nurture of children.

God gave us marriage as a holy mystery
in which a man and a woman are joined together,
and become one,
just as Christ is one with the church.

In marriage, husband and wife are called to a new way of life,
created, ordered, and blessed by God.
This way of life must not be entered into carelessly,
or from selfish motives,
but responsibly, and prayerfully.

We rejoice that marriage is given by God,
blessed by our Lord Jesus Christ,
and sustained by the Holy Spirit.
Therefore, let marriage be held in honor among all.

PRAYER

> *The minister says:*

Let us pray:

Gracious God, you are always faithful in your love for us,
Look mercifully upon _____ and _____,
who have come seeking your blessing.
Let your Holy Spirit rest upon them
so that with steadfast love
they may honor the promises they make this day,
through Jesus Christ our Savior.

Amen.

DECLARATIONS OF INTENT

> *The minister addresses the bride and groom individually:*

_____, having heard how God has created, ordered, and blessed
 the covenant of marriage,
do you affirm your desire and intention
to enter this covenant?

> *Answer:*

I do.

Or, if both are baptized, the following may be used.

_____ , in your baptism,
you have been called to union with Christ and the church.
Do you intend to honor this calling
through the covenant of marriage?

Answer:

I do.

AFFIRMATIONS OF THE FAMILIES

The minister may address the families of the bride and groom:

(Names of family members) _____ ,
do you give your blessing to _____ and _____ ,
and promise to do everything in your power to uphold them in their
   marriage?

Answer:

Or

We *(I)* give our *(my)* blessing   **We *(I)* do.**
and promise our *(my)* loving
   support.

The families may be seated.

AFFIRMATION OF THE CONGREGATION

*The minister may then address the congregation. The congregation
may stand.*

Will all of you witnessing these vows
do everything in your power to uphold _____ and _____ in their
   marriage?

Answer:

We will.

A psalm, hymn, spiritual, or other music may be used.

VOWS

The minister addresses the couple:

_____ and _____,
since it is your intention to marry,
join your right hands,
and with your promises
bind yourselves to each other as husband and wife.

The bride and groom face each other and join right hands. Then they shall say their vows to each other, in turn.

Or

The man says:

I, _____, take you, _____,
   to be my wife;
and I promise,
before God and these
   witnesses,
to be your loving and faithful
   husband;
in plenty and in want;
in joy and in sorrow;
in sickness and in health;
as long as we both shall live.

The man says:

Before God and these
   witnesses,
I, _____, take you, _____,
   to be my wife,
and I promise to love you,
and to be faithful to you,
as long as we both shall live.

The woman says:

I, _____ , take you, _____ ,
    to be my husband;
and I promise,
before God and these
    witnesses,
to be your loving and faithful
    wife;
in plenty and in want;
in joy and in sorrow;
in sickness and in health;
as long as we both shall live.

The woman says:

Before God and these
    witnesses,
I, _____ , take you, _____ ,
    to be my husband,
and I promise to love you,
and to be faithful to you
as long as we both shall live.

EXCHANGE OF RINGS (OR OTHER SYMBOLS)

If rings are to be exchanged, the minister says to the couple:

What do you bring as the sign of your promise?

When the rings are presented the minister may say the following prayer.

By your blessing, O God,
may these rings be to _____ and _____
symbols of unending love and faithfulness,
reminding them of the covenant they have made this day,
through Jesus Christ our Lord.

Amen.

The bride and groom shall exchange rings using these or other appropriate words.

Or

The one giving the ring says:

_____ , I give you this ring
as a sign of our covenant,
in the name of the Father,
and of the Son,
and of the Holy Spirit.

As each ring is given, the one giving the ring says:

This ring I give you,
as a sign of our constant faith
and abiding love,
in the name of the Father,
and of the Son,
and of the Holy Spirit.

The one receiving the ring says:

I receive this ring
as a sign of our covenant
in the name of the Father,
and of the Son,
and of the Holy Spirit.

PRAYER

The couple may kneel.

One of the following prayers, or a similar prayer, is said:

Let us pray:

Eternal God,
creator and preserver of all life,
author of salvation
and giver of all grace:
look with favor upon the world you have made and redeemed,
and especially upon _____ and _____ .

Give them wisdom and devotion in their common life,
that each may be to the other
a strength in need,
a comfort in sorrow,

a counselor in perplexity,
and a companion in joy.

Grant that their wills may be so knit together in your will,
and their spirits in your Spirit,
that they may grow in love and peace
with you and each other
all the days of their life.

Give them the courage,
when they hurt each other,
to recognize and confess their fault,
and the grace to seek your forgiveness,
and to forgive each other.

Make their life together
a sign of Christ's love to this sinful and broken world,
that unity may overcome estrangement,
forgiveness heal guilt,
and joy conquer despair.

Give them such fulfillment of their mutual love
that they may reach out in concern for others.

[Give to them, if it is your will,
the gift of children,
and the wisdom to bring them up
to know you, to love you,
and to serve you.]

Grant that all who have witnessed these vows today
may find their lives strengthened,
and that all who are married
may depart with their own promises renewed.

Enrich with your grace
all husbands and wives, parents and children,
that, loving and supporting one another,
they may serve those in need
and be a sign of your kingdom.

Grant that the bonds of our common humanity,
by which all your children are united one to another,
may be so transformed by your Spirit
that your peace and justice may fill the earth,
through Jesus Christ our Lord.

Amen.

Or

Eternal God,
without your grace no promise is sure.
Strengthen _____ and _____ with patience, kindness, gentleness,
and all other gifts of your Spirit,
so that they may fulfill the vows they have made.
Keep them faithful to each other and to you.
Fill them with such love and joy
that they may build a home of peace and welcome.
Guide them by your word
to serve you all their days.

Enable us all, O God,
in each of our homes and lives to do your will.
Enrich us with your grace
so that, encouraging and supporting one another,
we may serve those in need
and hasten the coming of peace, love, and justice on earth,
through Jesus Christ our Lord.

Amen.

When the Lord's Supper is not celebrated, the Lord's Prayer may be said or sung either here or after the prayer of thanksgiving.

When the Lord's Supper is celebrated, the Lord's Prayer shall follow the eucharistic prayer (the great prayer of thanksgiving).

Our Father in heaven,
  hallowed be your name,
  your kingdom come,
  your will be done,
    on earth as in heaven.
Give us today our daily bread.
Forgive us our sins
  as we forgive those
    who sin against us.
Save us from the time of trial
  and deliver us from evil.
For the kingdom, the power,
  and the glory are yours,
  now and forever. Amen.

Our Father, who art in heaven,
  hallowed be thy name,
  thy kingdom come,
  thy will be done,
    on earth as it is in heaven.
Give us this day our daily bread;
and forgive us our debts,
  as we forgive our debtors;
and lead us not into temptation,
  but deliver us from evil.
For thine is the kingdom,
  and the power, and the glory,
  forever. Amen.

ANNOUNCEMENT OF MARRIAGE

The minister addresses the congregation:

Before God
and in the presence of this congregation,
_____ and _____ have made their solemn vows to each other.
They have confirmed their promises by the joining of hands
[and by the giving and receiving of rings].
Therefore, I proclaim that they are now husband and wife.

Blessed be the Father and the Son and the Holy Spirit now and
  forever.

The minister joins the couple's right hands.

The congregation may join the minister saying:

**Those whom God has joined together
let no one separate.**

CHARGE TO THE COUPLE

The minister addresses the couple:

As God's own,
clothe yourselves with compassion,
kindness, and patience,
forgiving each other
as the Lord has forgiven you,
and crown all these things with love,
which binds everything together in perfect harmony.   *Col. 3:12–14*

Or

Whatever you do, in word or deed,
do everything in the name of the Lord Jesus,
giving thanks to God through him.   *Col. 3:17*

BLESSING OF THE COUPLE

The minister addresses the couple using one of the following blessings:

The grace of Christ attend you,
the love of God surround you,
the Holy Spirit keep you,
that you may live in faith,
abound in hope,
and grow in love,
both now and forevermore.

Amen.

Or

O gracious God,
we give you thanks for your tender love
in sending Jesus Christ
to dwell among us full of grace and truth,
and to make the way of the cross
to be the way of life.
We thank you also
for making holy the marriage of man and woman in his name.

By the power of your Holy Spirit,
pour out the abundance of your blessing
upon this man and this woman.
Defend them from every enemy.
Lead them into all peace.
Let their love for each other be
a seal upon their hearts,
a mantle about their shoulders,
and a crown upon their foreheads.
Bless them in their work and in their companionship;
in their sleeping and in their waking;
in their joys and in their sorrows;
in their life and in their death.
Finally, in your mercy,
bring them to that table
where your saints feast forever in your presence;
through Jesus Christ our Lord,
who with you and the Holy Spirit
lives and reigns, one God,
for ever and ever.

Amen.

A psalm, hymn, spiritual, anthem, or other appropriate music may be included here.

If the service is neither a Lord's Day service nor a service including the Lord's Supper, it may conclude at this point with a general blessing, and the wedding party may recess.

PRAYERS OF INTERCESSION

Prayers for worldwide and local concerns are offered.

GIVE THANKS TO GOD

If there is an offering, appropriate music may accompany the gathering of the people's offerings. As the offerings are brought forward, a doxology, hymn of praise, or spiritual is sung.

If the Lord's Supper is to be celebrated, the table is prepared with bread and wine. The bread and wine may be brought to the table or uncovered if already in place.

If the Lord's Supper is not to be celebrated, the service continues on page 47.

GREAT PRAYER OF THANKSGIVING

The minister leads the people in the great thanksgiving, using the following prayer (or Prayer A with Christian Marriage I or II variations in The Service for the Lord's Day *[Supplemental Liturgical Resource 1], liturgical text no. 183), introducing the prayer with the following dialogue, which may be sung or said:*

The Lord be with you.

And also with you.

Lift up your hearts.

We lift them to the Lord.

Let us give thanks to the Lord our God.

It is right to give our thanks and praise.

O holy Father, creator of all things,
and source of every blessing,
by your power and wisdom
you brought the universe into being,
and created us in your image.
You made us male and female
and gave us the freedom to be joined as husband and wife,
united in body and heart.
In your providence you gave us this earth,
to care for it and to delight in it.
With its bounty you preserve our life.

You called us to love and serve you,
but we turned against you
to follow our own ways.
In your mercy, you did not forsake us,
for your love is unfailing in every age.
You bound yourself to us with a covenant,
claiming us as your people,
and promising faithfulness as our God.
You made the union of husband and wife
a sign of your covenant with your people.

40   *Christian Marriage: Rite II*

Therefore, we praise you,
joining our voices with choirs of angels,
and with all the faithful of every time and place,
who forever sing to the glory of your name:

**Holy, holy, holy Lord, God of power and might,
heaven and earth are full of your glory.
   Hosanna in the highest.**

**Blessed is he who comes in the name of the Lord.
   Hosanna in the highest.**

Blessed are you, O Lord our God,
for out of your great love for the world,
you gave your only Son to be our Savior.
By the power of the Holy Spirit,
Christ was born as one of us,
shared our joys and sorrows,
and offered his life in perfect obedience and trust.
By his death,
Christ delivered us from our sins, reconciling us to you.
Rising from the tomb,
he gave us new and abundant life,
and offered healing for every human relationship.
By his sacrificial love,
Christ sanctified the church to be his holy bride.
Even now he is preparing the wedding banquet.

> *The words of institution may be said here or in relation to the breaking of the bread.*

[We give you thanks that on the night before he died,
Jesus took bread.
After giving thanks to you, he broke it,
and gave it to his disciples, saying,
"Take, eat.
This is my body, given for you.
Do this in remembrance of me."

In the same way he took the cup, saying,
"This cup is the new covenant sealed in my blood,
shed for you for the forgiveness of sins.
Do this in remembrance of me."]

In remembrance of your mighty acts in Jesus Christ,
we take from your creation this bread and this wine
and celebrate his death and resurrection,
as we await the day of his coming.
Accept this our sacrifice of praise and thanksgiving,
as a living and holy offering of ourselves,
dedicated to your service,
that our lives may proclaim the mystery of faith.

Christ has died,
Christ is risen,
Christ will come again.

Gracious God,
Pour out your Holy Spirit upon us,
and upon these your gifts of bread and wine,
that the bread we break
and the cup we bless
may be the communion of the body and blood of Christ.
By your Spirit make us one with Christ,
and one with all who share this feast.

Give _____ and _____ the spirit of love and peace,
that they may become one in heart and mind,
and rejoice together in your gift of marriage.
Let their love for each other
witness to your divine love in the world.
Strengthen us and your church in every place
to serve you faithfully,
and to proclaim your justice, joy, and peace to all the world,
until we feast in glory
at the marriage supper of the Lamb,
Jesus Christ our Lord.

Through Christ, with Christ, in Christ,
in the unity of the Holy Spirit,
all glory and honor, praise and adoration are yours,
eternal Father,
now and forever.

Amen.

The Lord's Prayer is sung or said.

Our Father in heaven,
  hallowed be your name,
  your kingdom come,
  your will be done,
    on earth as in heaven.
Give us today our daily bread.
Forgive us our sins
  as we forgive those
    who sin against us.
Save us from the time of trial
  and deliver us from evil.
For the kingdom, the power,
  and the glory are yours,
  now and forever. Amen.

Our Father, who art in heaven,
  hallowed be thy name,
  thy kingdom come,
  thy will be done,
    on earth as it is in heaven.
Give us this day our daily bread;
and forgive us our debts,
  as we forgive our debtors;
and lead us not into temptation,
  but deliver us from evil.
For thine is the kingdom,
  and the power, and the glory,
  forever. Amen.

If the words of institution were included in the great prayer of thanksgiving, the minister holds the bread in full view of the people, saying:

Because there is one loaf,
we, many as we are, are one
   body;
for it is one loaf of which we all
   partake.

The minister breaks the bread in full view of the congregation.

When we break the bread,
is it not a sharing in the body of
   Christ?

The minister lifts the cup.

When we give thanks over the
   cup,
is it not a sharing in the blood of
   Christ?
                    (1 Cor. 10:16–17)

If the words of institution were not included in the great prayer of thanksgiving, the minister breaks the bread in the presence of the people, saying:

The Lord Jesus, on the night of
   his arrest, took bread,
and after giving thanks to God,
he broke it and said,
"This is my body, given for you.
Do this in remembrance of me."

The minister lifts the cup, saying:

In the same way, he took the
   cup after supper, saying,
"This cup is the new covenant
   sealed in my blood.
Whenever you drink it,
do it in remembrance of me."

Every time you eat this bread
   and drink this cup,
you proclaim the death of the
   Lord,
until he comes.
(1 Cor. 11:23–26; Luke 22:19–20)

Holding out both the bread and the cup to the people, the minister says:

The gifts of God
for the people of God.

COMMUNION OF THE PEOPLE

As the bread and wine are given, the following words may be said:

The bread of heaven.

Amen.

The cup of salvation.

Amen.

GO IN GOD'S NAME

PRAYER

After all are served, the following prayer may be offered by the minister or by all:

Loving God,
we thank you that you have fed us in this holy meal,
united us with Christ,
and given us a foretaste of the marriage feast of the Lamb.
So strengthen us in your service
that our daily living may show our thanks,
through Jesus Christ our Lord.

Amen.

PRAISE

A psalm, hymn of praise, or spiritual is sung.

CHARGE

A charge to the people may be said:

Go out into the world in peace;
have courage;
hold on to what is good;
return no one evil for evil;
strengthen the fainthearted;   *1 Cor. 16:13*
support the weak, and help the suffering;   *2 Tim. 2:1*
honor everyone;   *Eph. 6:10*
love and serve the Lord,   *1 Thess. 5:13–22*
rejoicing in the power of the Holy Spirit.   *1 Peter 2:17*

      Or

Go in peace
to love and serve the Lord.

BENEDICTION

The people are dismissed with these or other words of Scripture:

The Lord bless you and keep you.
The Lord be kind and gracious to you.
The Lord look upon you with favor
and give you peace.   *Num. 6:24–26*

Amen.

When the Lord's Supper is omitted, the service continues from page 40, and concludes in the following manner:

PRAYER OF THANKSGIVING

The people are led in prayer:

The Lord be with you.

And also with you.

Lift up your hearts.

We lift them to the Lord.

Let us give thanks to the Lord our God.

It is right to give our thanks and praise.

The minister continues, using one of the following prayers or a similar prayer.

O holy Father, creator of all things
and source of every blessing,
by your power and wisdom
you brought the universe into being,
and created us in your image.
You made us male and female,
and gave us the freedom to be joined as husband and wife,
united in body and heart.
In your providence you gave us this earth,
to care for it and to delight in it.
With its bounty you preserve our life.

You called us to love and serve you,
but we turned against you
to follow our own ways.
In your mercy, you did not forsake us,
for your love is unfailing in every age.
You bound yourself to us with a covenant,
claiming us as your people,
and promising faithfulness as our God.
You made the union of husband and wife
a sign of your covenant with your people.

We praise you, O Lord our God,
for out of your great love for the world,
you gave your only Son to be our Savior.
By the power of the Holy Spirit,
Christ was born as one of us,
shared our joys and sorrows,
and offered his life in perfect obedience and trust.
By his death,
Christ delivered us from our sins, reconciling us to you.
Rising from the tomb,
he gave us new and abundant life,
and offered healing for every human relationship.
By his sacrificial love,
Christ sanctified the church to be his holy bride.
Even now Christ is preparing the wedding banquet.

Give _____ and _____ the spirit of love and peace,
that they may become one in heart and mind,
and rejoice together in your gift of marriage.
Let their love for each other
witness to your divine love in the world.
Strengthen us and your church in every place
to serve you faithfully,
and to proclaim your justice, joy, and peace to all the world,
until we feast in glory
at the marriage supper of the Lamb.

Through Christ, with Christ, in Christ,
in the unity of the Holy Spirit,
all glory and honor, praise and adoration are yours,
eternal Father,
now and forever.

Amen.

Or

Almighty and merciful God,
from whom comes every good and every perfect gift,
we praise you for your mercies,
for your goodness that has created us,
your grace that has sustained us,
your discipline that has corrected us,
your patience that has borne with us,
and your love that has redeemed us.

Help us to love you,
and to be thankful for all your gifts
by serving you and delighting to do your will,
through Jesus Christ our Lord.

Amen.

The Lord's Prayer is sung or said here, if it has not been used earlier.

Our Father in heaven,
  hallowed be your name,
  your kingdom come,
  your will be done,
    on earth as in heaven.
Give us today our daily bread.
Forgive us our sins
  as we forgive those
    who sin against us.
Save us from the time of trial
  and deliver us from evil.
For the kingdom, the power,
  and the glory are yours,
  now and forever. Amen.

Our Father, who art in heaven,
  hallowed be thy name,
  thy kingdom come,
  thy will be done,
    on earth as it is in heaven.
Give us this day our daily bread;
and forgive us our debts,
  as we forgive our debtors;
and lead us not into temptation,
  but deliver us from evil.
For thine is the kingdom,
  and the power, and the glory,
    forever. Amen.

GO IN GOD'S NAME

PRAISE

A psalm, hymn of praise, or spiritual is sung.

CHARGE

A charge to the people may be said:

Go out into the world in peace;
have courage;
hold on to what is good;
return no one evil for evil;
strengthen the fainthearted;
support the weak, and help the suffering;   *1 Cor. 16:13*
honor everyone;   *2 Tim. 2:1*
love and serve the Lord,   *1 Thess. 5:13–22*
rejoicing in the power of the Holy Spirit.   *1 Peter 2:17*

> *Or*

Go in peace,
to love and serve the Lord.

BENEDICTION

The people are dismissed with these or other words of Scripture:

The Lord bless you and keep you.
The Lord be kind and gracious to you.
The Lord look upon you with favor
and give you peace.   *Num. 6:24–26*

Amen.

OUTLINE OF
CHRISTIAN MARRIAGE: RITE III

A Service of Christian Marriage
for Those Previously Married in a Civil Ceremony

Entrance
Sentences of Scripture
Statement on the Gift of Marriage
Prayer
Declarations of Intent
Affirmation of the Families
Affirmation of the Congregation
(Psalm, Hymn, or Spiritual)
Scripture and Sermon
(Psalm, Hymn, or Spiritual)
Vows
Prayer and Lord's Prayer
Charge to the Couple
Benediction
(Psalm, Hymn, Spiritual, or Anthem)

CHRISTIAN MARRIAGE: RITE III
A Service of Christian Marriage
for Those Previously Married in a Civil Ceremony

This rite is designed to allow those who have been previously married in a civil ceremony to make the promises of Christian marriage before the witness of the church and in the context of Christian worship. The service may be used independently, or, with certain alterations, incorporated into the Service for the Lord's Day.

ENTRANCE

At the appointed time, the couple present themselves and stand in front of the minister. The families may stand with the couple. A psalm, hymn, spiritual, or anthem may be sung, or instrumental music may be played as they enter.

SENTENCES OF SCRIPTURE

Either before or after the entrance, the people are called to worship with these or other words from Scripture:

God is love,
and those who abide in love
abide in God,
and God abides in them.   *1 John 4:16*

    Or

This is the day the Lord has made.
Let us rejoice and be glad in it.   *Psalm 118:24*

STATEMENT ON THE GIFT OF MARRIAGE

The minister shall say:

_____ and _____
are married according to the law of the state,
and they have spoken vows pledging loyalty and love.
Now, in the presence of God and the church,

they have come to reaffirm those vows
and in faith to confess their common purpose in the Lord.
We have gathered to witness their promises to each other,
to surround them with our prayers,
to give thanks to God for the gift of marriage,
and to ask God's blessing upon them,
so that they may be strengthened for their life together
and nurtured in their love for God.

God created us male and female,
and gave us marriage
so that husband and wife may help and comfort each other,
living faithfully together in plenty and in want,
in joy and in sorrow,
in sickness and in health,
throughout all their days.

God gave us marriage
for the full expression of the love between a man and a woman.
In marriage a woman and a man belong to each other,
and with affection and tenderness
freely give themselves to each other.

God gave us marriage
for the well-being of human society,
for the ordering of family life,
and for the birth and nurture of children.

God gave us marriage as a holy mystery
in which a man and a woman are joined together,
and become one,
just as Christ is one with the church.

In marriage, husband and wife are called to a new way of life,
created, ordered, and blessed by God.
It is to be lived prayerfully,
and in joyful obedience to Christ.

We rejoice that marriage is given by God,
blessed by our Lord Jesus Christ,
and sustained by the Holy Spirit.
Therefore, let marriage be held in honor among all.

PRAYER

The minister says:

Let us pray:

Gracious God, you are always faithful in vour love for us.
Look mercifully upon _____ and _____,
who have come seeking your blessing.
Let your Holy Spirit rest upon them
so that with steadfast love
they may honor the promises they make this day,
through Jesus Christ our Savior.

Amen.

DECLARATIONS OF INTENT

The minister addresses the man and woman individually:

_____, you have heard how God has created, ordered, and blessed
the covenant of marriage.
Now in the presence of God and the church,
do you wish to affirm the vows of Christian marriage?

Answer:

I do.

AFFIRMATIONS OF THE FAMILIES

The minister may address the families of the couple:

(Names of family members) _____,
do you give your blessing to _____ and _____,
and promise to do everything in your power to uphold them in their
marriage?

Answer:

Or

We *(I)* **give our** *(my)* **blessing**   **We** *(I)* **do.**
and promise our *(my)* **loving**
   support.

> *The families may be seated.*

AFFIRMATION OF THE CONGREGATION

> *The minister may then address the congregation. The congregation may stand.*

Will all of you witnessing these vows
do everything in your power to uphold _____ and _____ in their
   marriage?

> *Answer:*

We will.

> *A psalm, hymn, spiritual, or anthem may be sung.*

SCRIPTURE AND SERMON

> *The following, or a similar prayer for illumination, may be said:*

God of mercy,
you have never broken your covenant with us,
and you free us to live together
in the power of your faithful love.
Amid all the changing words of our generation,
may we hear your eternal Word that does not change.
Then may we respond to your gracious promises
with faithful and obedient lives;
through our Lord Jesus Christ.
Amen.

> *Scripture shall be read.*
>
> *A brief sermon may follow.*
>
> *A psalm, hymn, spiritual, or other music may be used.*

Vows

The minister addresses the couple:

_____ and _____ ,
join your right hands,
and in faith make your promises to each other
as husband and wife.

> *The couple face each other and join right hands. Then, in turn, they shall say their vows.*

Or

The man says:	*The man says:*

_____ , you are my wife,
and I promise,
before God and these
    witnesses,
to be your loving and faithful
    husband;
in plenty and in want;
in joy and in sorrow;
in sickness and in health;
as long as we both shall live.

_____ , you are my wife.
Before God and these
    witnesses,
I promise to love you,
and to be faithful to you,
as long as we both shall live.

The woman says:

The woman says:

_____ , you are my husband,
and I promise,
before God and these
    witnesses,
to be your loving and faithful
    wife;
in plenty and in want;
in joy and in sorrow;
in sickness and in health;
as long as we both shall live.

_____ , you are my husband.
Before God and these
    witnesses,
I promise to love you,
and to be faithful to you
as long as we both shall live.

PRAYER

The couple may kneel.

One of the following prayers, or a similar prayer, is said:

Let us pray:

Eternal God,
creator and preserver of all life,
author of salvation
and giver of all grace:
look with favor upon the world you have made and redeemed,
and especially upon _____ and _____ .

Give them wisdom and devotion in their common life,
that each may be to the other
a strength in need,
a comfort in sorrow,
a counselor in perplexity,
and a companion in joy.

Grant that their wills may be so knit together in your will,
and their spirits in your Spirit,
that they may grow in love and peace
with you and each other
all the days of their life.

Give them the courage,
when they hurt each other,
to recognize and confess their fault,
and the grace to seek your forgiveness,
and to forgive each other.

Make their life together
a sign of Christ's love to this sinful and broken world,
that unity may overcome estrangement,
forgiveness heal guilt,
and joy conquer despair.

Give them such fulfillment of their mutual love
that they may reach out in concern for others.

[Give to them, if it is your will,
the gift of children,

and the wisdom to bring them up
to know you, to love you,
and to serve you.]

Grant that all who have witnessed these vows today
may find their lives strengthened,
and that all who are married
may depart with their own promises renewed.

Enrich with your grace
all husbands and wives, parents and children,
that, loving and supporting one another,
they may serve those in need
and be a sign of your kingdom.

Grant that the bonds of our common humanity,
by which all your children are united one to another,
may be so transformed by your Spirit
that your peace and justice may fill the earth,
through Jesus Christ our Lord.

Amen.

Or

Eternal God,
without your grace no promise is sure.
Strengthen _____ and _____ with patience, kindness, gentleness,
and all other gifts of your Spirit,
so that they may fulfill the vows they have made.
Keep them faithful to each other and to you.
Fill them with such love and joy
that they may build a home of peace and welcome.
Guide them by your word
to serve you all their days.

Enable us all, O God,
in each of our homes and lives to do your will.
Enrich us with your grace
so that, encouraging and supporting one another,
we may serve those in need
and hasten the coming of peace, love, and justice on earth,
through Jesus Christ our Lord.

Amen.

The Lord's Prayer may be said or sung.

Our Father in heaven,
   hallowed be your name,
   your kingdom come,
   your will be done,
     on earth as in heaven.
Give us today our daily bread.
Forgive us our sins
   as we forgive those
     who sin against us.
Save us from the time of trial
   and deliver us from evil.
For the kingdom, the power,
     and the glory are yours,
   now and forever. Amen.

Our Father, who art in heaven,
   hallowed be thy name,
   thy kingdom come,
   thy will be done,
     on earth as it is in heaven.
Give us this day our daily bread;
and forgive us our debts,
   as we forgive our debtors;
and lead us not into temptation,
   but deliver us from evil.
For thine is the kingdom,
   and the power, and the glory,
   forever. Amen.

The minister joins the couple's right hands.

The congregation may join the minister saying:

**Those whom God has joined together
let no one separate.**

CHARGE TO THE COUPLE

The minister addresses the couple:

As God's own,
clothe yourselves with compassion,
kindness, and patience,
forgiving each other
as the Lord has forgiven you,
and crown all these things with love,
which binds everything together in perfect harmony.   *Col. 3:12–14*

   Or

Whatever you do, in word or deed,
do everything in the name of the Lord Jesus,
giving thanks to God through him.   *Col. 3:17*

BENEDICTION

The minister addresses the couple and the congregation:

The Lord bless you and keep you.
The Lord be kind and gracious to you.
The Lord look upon you with favor
and give you peace.   *Num. 6:24–26*

Amen.

Or

The grace of Christ attend you,
the love of God surround you,
the Holy Spirit keep you,
that you may live in faith,
abound in hope,
and grow in love,
both now and forevermore.

Amen.

A psalm, hymn, spiritual, or anthem may be sung, or instrumental music may be played as the wedding party leaves.

ALTERNATE LITURGICAL TEXTS

This section provides liturgical texts that may be substituted for portions of the marriage rite.

SENTENCES OF SCRIPTURE

1.
Give thanks to the Lord,
for the Lord is good.

God's love endures forever.   *Ps. 106:1 and elsewhere*

2.
Trust in the Lord, and do good;
so you will dwell in the land, and enjoy security.
Take delight in the Lord,
and the Lord will give you the desires of your heart.   *Ps. 37:3–4*

3.
O come, let us sing to the Lord

and shout with joy to the rock of our salvation!

Let us come into God's presence with thanksgiving,

singing joyful songs of praise.   *Ps. 95:1–2*

STATEMENT ON THE GIFT OF MARRIAGE

Unless the Lord builds the house,
its builders will have toiled in vain.

Our help is in the name of the Lord,
maker of heaven and earth.

Beloved, we have come together in the house of God
to celebrate the marriage of _____ and _____,
in the assurance that the Lord Jesus Christ,
whose power was revealed at the wedding in Cana of Galilee,
is present with us here
in all his power and love.

Marriage is provided
as part of God's loving purpose for humanity
since the beginning of creation.
Jesus said,
"The Creator made them from the beginning male and female.
For this reason a man shall leave his father and mother,
and be made one with his wife:
and the two shall become one flesh."

Marriage is enriched by God
for all who have faith in the gospel,
for through the saving grace of Christ
and the renewal of the Holy Spirit
husband and wife can love one another
as Christ loves them.

Marriage is thus a gift and calling of God
and is not to be undertaken lightly
or from selfish motives
but with reverence and dedication,
with faith in the enabling power of Christ,
and with due awareness of the purpose
for which it is appointed by God.

Marriage is appointed
that there may be lifelong companionship,
comfort and joy between husband and wife.

It is appointed as the right and proper setting
for the full expression of physical love between man and woman.

It is appointed for the ordering of family life,
where children, who are also God's gift to us,
may enjoy the security of love
and the heritage of faith.

It is appointed for the well-being of human society,
which can be stable and happy
only where the marriage bond is honored and upheld.

PRAYERS

The following prayer may be used instead of the prayer that appears on pp. 13, 30, 54.

O God,
you have made the covenant of marriage a holy mystery,
a symbol of Christ's love for the church.
Hear our prayers for _____ and _____ .
With faith in you and in each other,
they pledge their love today.
May their lives always bear witness to the reality of that love.
We ask this through your Son,
our Lord Jesus Christ.

Amen.

Any of the following prayers may be used instead of the prayer that appears on pp. 18, 34, 57.

A.
Let us bless God for all the gifts in which we rejoice today.

Silent prayer.

Lord God,
constant in mercy, great in faithfulness:
With praise
we recall your acts of unfailing love for the human family,
for the house of Israel,
and for your people the church.

We bless you for the joy which your servants _____ and _____
have found in each other,
and pray that you give to them and to us such a sense of your
constant love
that we may employ all our strength to praise you,
whose work alone holds true
and endures forever.

Amen.

Let us pray for _____ and _____ in their life together.

Silent prayer.

Faithful Lord, source of love,
Pour down your grace upon _____ and _____,
that they may fulfill the vows they have made this day
and reflect your steadfast love
in their lifelong faithfulness to each other.
As members with them of the body of Christ,
use us to support their life together;
and from your great store of strength
give them power and patience,
affection and understanding,
courage, and love toward you,
toward each other,
and toward the world,
that they may continue together in mutual growth
according to your will in Jesus Christ our Lord.

Amen.

Other intercessions may be offered.

Let us pray for all families throughout the world.

Silent prayer.

Gracious God,
you bless the family and renew your people.
Enrich husbands and wives,
parents and children
more and more with your grace,
that, strengthening and supporting each other,
they may serve those in need
and be a sign of the fulfillment of your perfect kingdom,
where, with your Son Jesus Christ
and the Holy Spirit,
you live and reign,
one God forever.

Amen.

B.

Almighty God,
giver of life and love,
bless _____ and _____,
whom you have now joined in Christian marriage.
Grant them wisdom and devotion in their life together,
that each may be to the other a strength in need,
a comfort in sorrow, and a companion in joy.
So unite their wills in your will,
and their spirits in your Spirit,
that they live and grow together in love and peace
all the days of their life;
through Jesus Christ our Lord.

Amen.

C.

Almighty God,
you have created all humankind to glorify you in body and in spirit.
Give these your children joy in each other
as living temples of the Holy Spirit,
and bring them by this joy
to know and share in your creative and redeeming love;
through Jesus Christ our Lord.

Amen.

D.

Eternal God,
in holy marriage you make your servants one.
May their life together
witness to your love in this troubled world;
may unity overcome division,
forgiveness heal injury,
and joy triumph over sorrow;
through Jesus Christ our Lord.

Amen.

SCRIPTURE READINGS

SCRIPTURE READINGS

The following readings are particularly appropriate for the marriage service (pp. 16, 28, 55). All readings are from the Revised Standard Version of the Bible.

Old Testament

Then the LORD God said, "It is not good that the man should be alone; I will make him a helper fit for him." So out of the ground the LORD God formed every beast of the field and every bird of the air, and brought them to the man to see what he would call them; and whatever the man called every living creature, that was its name. The man gave names to all cattle, and to the birds of the air, and to every beast of the field; but for the man there was not found a helper fit for him. So the LORD God caused a deep sleep to fall upon the man, and while he slept took one of his ribs and closed up its place with flesh; and the rib which the LORD God had taken from the man he made into a woman and brought her to the man. Then the man said,

> "This at last is bone of my bones
>   and flesh of my flesh;
> she shall be called Woman,
>   because she was taken out of Man."

Therefore a man leaves his father and his mother and cleaves to his wife, and they become one flesh.   *Genesis 2:18–24*

Set me as a seal upon your heart,
   as a seal upon your arm;
for love is strong as death,
   jealousy is cruel as the grave.
Its flashes are flashes of fire,
   a most vehement flame.
Many waters cannot quench love,
   neither can floods drown it.
If a man offered for love
   all the wealth of his house,
   it would be utterly scorned.   *Song of Solomon 8:6–7*

Let not loyalty and faithfulness forsake you;
   bind them about your neck,
   write them on the tablet of your heart.
So you will find favor and good repute
   in the sight of God and man.

Trust in the LORD with your heart,
   and do not rely on your own insight.
In all your ways acknowledge him,
   and he will make straight your paths.   *Proverbs 3:3–6*

Your Maker is your husband,
   the LORD of hosts is his name;
and the Holy One of Israel is your Redeemer,
   the God of the whole earth he is called.
For the LORD has called you
   like a wife forsaken and grieved in spirit,
like a wife of youth when she is cast off,
   says your God.
For a brief moment I forsook you,
   but with great compassion I will gather you.
In overflowing wrath for a moment
   I hid my face from you,
but with everlasting love I will have compassion on you,
   says the LORD, your Redeemer.   *Isaiah 54:5–8*

   Other appropriate Old Testament readings include:

     Genesis 1:26–31
     Jeremiah 31:31–34

Psalms

May God be gracious to us and bless us
  and make his face to shine upon us,
that thy way may be known upon earth,
  thy saving power among all nations.
Let the peoples praise thee, O God;
  let all the peoples praise thee!

Let the nations be glad and sing for joy,
  for thou dost judge the peoples with equity
  and guide the nations upon earth.
Let the peoples praise thee, O God;
  let all the peoples praise thee!

The earth has yielded its increase;
  God, our God, has blessed us.
God has blessed us;
  let all the ends of the earth fear him!   *Psalm 67*

O come, let us sing to the LORD;
  let us make a joyful noise to the rock of our salvation!
Let us come into his presence with thanksgiving;
  let us make a joyful noise to him with songs of praise!
For the LORD is a great God,
  and a great King above all gods.
In his hand are the depths of the earth;
  the heights of the mountains are his also.
The sea is his, for he made it;
  for his hands formed the dry land.

O come, let us worship and bow down,
  let us kneel before the LORD, our Maker!
For he is our God,
  and we are the people of his pasture,
  and the sheep of his hand.

O that today you would hearken to his voice!   *Psalm 95:1–7*

Make a joyful noise to the LORD, all the lands!
  Serve the LORD with gladness!
  Come into his presence with singing!

Know that the LORD is God!
    It is he that made us, and we are his;
    we are his people, and the sheep of his pasture.

Enter his gates with thanksgiving,
    and his courts with praise!
    Give thanks to him, bless his name!

For the LORD is good;
    his steadfast love endures for ever,
    and his faithfulness to all generations.   *Psalm 100*

Bless the LORD, O my soul,
    and all that is within me, bless his holy name!
Bless the LORD, O my soul,
    and forget not all his benefits,
who forgives all your iniquity,
    who heals all your diseases,
who redeems your life from the Pit,
    who crowns you with steadfast love and mercy,
who satisfies you with good as long as you live
    so that your youth is renewed like the eagle's.

As for man, his days are like grass;
    he flourishes like a flower of the field;
for the wind passes over it, and it is gone,
    and its place knows it no more.
But the steadfast love of the LORD is from everlasting to everlasting
    upon those who fear him,
    and his righteousness to children's children,
to those who keep his covenant
    and remember to do his commandments.   *Psalm 103:1–5, 15–18*

O give thanks to the LORD, for he is good,
    for his steadfast love endures for ever.
O give thanks to the God of gods,
    for his steadfast love endures for ever.
O give thanks to the Lord of lords,
    for his steadfast love endures for ever;

to him who alone does great wonders,
    for his steadfast love endures for ever;
to him who by understanding made the heavens,
    for his steadfast love endures for ever;

to him who spread out the earth upon the waters,
    for his steadfast love endures for ever;
to him who made the great lights,
    for his steadfast love endures for ever;
the sun to rule over the day,
    for his steadfast love endures for ever;
the moon and stars to rule over the night
    for his steadfast love endures for ever.

O give thanks to the God of heaven,
    for his steadfast love endures for ever.   *Psalm 136:1–9, 26*

I will extol thee, my God and King,
    and bless thy name for ever and ever.
Every day I will bless thee,
    and praise thy name for ever and ever.
Great is the LORD, and greatly to be praised,
    and his greatness is unsearchable.

One generation shall laud thy works to another,
    and shall declare thy mighty acts.
On the glorious splendor of thy majesty,
    and on thy wondrous works, I will meditate.
Men shall proclaim the might of thy terrible acts,
    and I will declare thy greatness.
They shall pour forth the fame of thy abundant goodness,
    and shall sing aloud of thy righteousness.

The LORD is gracious and merciful,
    slow to anger and abounding in steadfast love.
The LORD is good to all,
    and his compassion is over all that he has made.

All thy works shall give thanks to thee, O LORD,
    and all thy saints shall bless thee!
They shall speak of the glory of thy kingdom,
    and tell of thy power,
to make known to the sons of men thy mighty deeds,
    and the glorious splendor of thy kingdom.
Thy kingdom is an everlasting kingdom,
    and thy dominion endures throughout all generations.

The LORD is faithful in all his words,
    and gracious in all his deeds.

The LORD upholds all who are falling,
and raises up all who are bowed down.
The eyes of all look to thee,
and thou givest them their food in due season.
Thou openest thy hand,
thou satisfiest the desire of every living thing.
The LORD is just in all his ways,
and kind in all his doings.
The LORD is near to all who call upon him,
to all who call upon him in truth.
He fulfils the desire of all who fear him,
he also hears their cry, and saves them.
The LORD preserves all who love him;
but all the wicked he will destroy.

My mouth will speak the praise of the LORD,
and let all flesh bless his holy name for ever and ever.   *Psalm 145*

Other appropriate psalms include:

Psalm 8	*Psalm 128*
Psalm 117	*Psalm 148*
Psalm 121	*Psalm 150*

Epistles

I appeal to you therefore, brethren, by the mercies of God, to present your bodies as a living sacrifice, holy and acceptable to God, which is your spiritual worship. Do not be conformed to this world but be transformed by the renewal of your mind, that you may prove what is the will of God, what is good and acceptable and perfect.

Let love be genuine; hate what is evil, hold fast to what is good; love one another with brotherly affection; outdo one another in showing honor. Never flag in zeal, be aglow with the Spirit, serve the Lord. Rejoice in your hope, be patient in tribulation, be constant in prayer. Contribute to the needs of the saints, practice hospitality.

Bless those who persecute you; bless and do not curse them. Rejoice with those who rejoice, weep with those who weep. Live in harmony with one another; do not be haughty, but associate with the lowly; never be conceited. Repay no one evil for evil, but take thought for what is noble in the sight of all. If possible, so far as it depends upon you, live peaceably with all.   *Romans 12:1-2, 9-18*

If I speak in the tongues of men and of angels, but have not love, I am a noisy gong or a clanging cymbal. And if I have prophetic powers and understand all mysteries and all knowledge, and if I have all faith, so as to remove mountains, but have not love, I am nothing. If I give away all I have, and if I deliver my body to be burned, but have not love, I gain nothing.

Love is patient and kind; love is not jealous or boastful; it is not arrogant or rude. Love does not insist on its own way; it is not irritable or resentful, it does not rejoice at wrong, but rejoices in the right. Love bears all things, believes all things, hopes all things, endures all things.

Love never ends; as for prophecies, they will pass away; as for tongues, they will cease; as for knowledge, it will pass away. For our knowledge is imperfect and our prophecy is imperfect; but when the perfect comes, the imperfect will pass away. When I was a child, I spoke like child, I thought like a child, I reasoned like a child; when I became a man, I gave up childish ways. For now we see in a mirror dimly, but then face to face. Now I know in part; then I shall understand fully, even as I have been fully understood. So faith, hope, love abide, these three; but the greatest of these is love.

1 Corinthians 13:1–13

Be subject to one another out of reverence for Christ. Wives, be subject to your husbands, as to the Lord. For the husband is the head of the wife as Christ is the head of the church, his body, and is himself its Savior. As the church is subject to Christ, so let wives also be subject in everything to their husbands. Husbands, love your wives, as Christ loved the church and gave himself up for her, that he might sanctify her, having cleansed her by the washing of water with the word, that he might present the church to himself in splendor, without spot or wrinkle or any such thing, that she might be holy and without blemish. Even so husbands should love their wives as their own bodies. He who loves his wife loves himself. For no man ever hates his own flesh, but nourishes and cherishes it, as Christ does the church, because we are members of his body. "For this reason a man shall leave his father and mother and be joined to his wife, and the two shall become one flesh." This mystery is a profound one, and I am saying that it refers to Christ and the church; however, let each one of you love his wife as himself, and let the wife see that she respects her husband.

Ephesians 5:21–33

Gospels

Seeing the crowds, he went up on the mountain, and when he sat down his disciples came to him. And he opened his mouth and taught them, saying:

"Blessed are the poor in spirit, for theirs is the kingdom of heaven.

"Blessed are those who mourn, for they shall be comforted.

"Blessed are the meek, for they shall inherit the earth.

"Blessed are those who hunger and thirst for righteousness, for they shall be satisfied.

"Blessed are the merciful, for they shall obtain mercy.

"Blessed are the pure in heart, for they shall see God.

"Blessed are the peacemakers, for they shall be called sons of God.

"Blessed are those who are persecuted for righteousness' sake, for theirs is the kingdom of heaven." *Matthew 5:1–10*

"You are the salt of the earth; but if salt has lost its taste, how shall its saltness be restored? It is no longer good for anything except to be thrown out and trodden under foot by men.

"You are the light of the world. A city set on a hill cannot be hid. Nor do men light a lamp and put it under a bushel, but on a stand, and it gives light to all in the house. Let your light so shine before men, that they may see your good works and give glory to your Father who is in heaven." *Matthew 5:13–16*

And one of them, a lawyer, asked him a question, to test him. "Teacher, which is the great commandment in the law?" And he said to him, "You shall love the Lord your God with all your heart, and with all your soul, and with all your mind. This is the great and first commandment. And a second is like it, You shall love your neighbor as yourself. On these two commandments depend all the law and the prophets." *Matthew 22:35–40*

"From the beginning of creation, 'God made them male and female.' 'For this reason a man shall leave his father and mother and be joined to his wife, and the two shall become one flesh.' So they are no longer two but one flesh. What therefore God has joined together, let not man put asunder." *Mark 10:6–9*

"I am the true vine, and my Father is the vinedresser. Every branch of mine that bears no fruit, he takes away, and every branch that does bear fruit he prunes, that it may bear more fruit. You are already made clean by the word which I have spoken to you. Abide in me, and I in you. As the branch cannot bear fruit by itself, unless it abides in the vine, neither can you, unless you abide in me. I am the vine, you are the branches. He who abides in me, and I in him, he it is that bears much fruit, for apart from me you can do nothing. If a man does not abide in me, he is cast forth as a branch and withers; and the branches are gathered, thrown into the fire and burned. If you abide in me, and my words abide in you, ask whatever you will, and it shall be done for you. By this my Father is glorified, that you bear much fruit, and so prove to be my disciples. As the Father has loved me, so have I loved you; abide in my love. If you keep my commandments, you will abide in my love, just as I have kept my Father's commandments and abide in his love. These things I have spoken to you, that my joy may be in you, and that your joy may be full.

"This is my commandment, that you love one another as I have loved you. Greater love has no man than this, that a man lay down his life for his friends. You are my friends if you do what I command you. No longer do I call you servants, for the servant does not know what his master is doing; but I have called you friends, for all that I have heard from my Father I have made known to you. You did not choose me, but I chose you and appointed you that you should go and bear fruit and that your fruit should abide; so that whatever you ask the Father in my name, he may give it to you. This I command you, to love one another."   *John 15:1–17*

Other appropriate readings from the New Testament include:

Matthew 19:3–6   Colossians 3:12–17   Revelation 19:1, 5–9
John 2:1–11   1 John 4:7–12

COMMENTARY
ON
AN ORDER FOR
CHRISTIAN MARRIAGE

1

THE MARRIAGE SERVICE AS WORSHIP

History

The church has not always been involved in weddings. Historically, the marriage service, or rite, was a latecomer into the sanctuary. While the relationship between a husband and a wife has always been theologically and ethically important to Christians, the wedding itself was not a part of the church's worship for several centuries. Generally speaking, early Christians married according to the laws and practices of the Roman Empire, which involved legal and civil ceremonies usually performed in homes.[1] The character of the marriage was of concern to the church, but the wedding ceremony was the business of the state. The Roman civil wedding contained many customs that are still observed today, such as the declaration of consent, the joining of hands, a wedding feast with a symbolic cake, and the exchanging of gifts.[2]

The church's involvement in the marriage ceremony has grown steadily over the years. Initially the church was involved only to the extent that the clergy encouraged Christians to marry within the faith and provided pastoral guidance to prospective marriage partners. Later it appears that a specifically Christian service of blessing was added to the end of the civil ceremony. This brief supplement to the state's service gradually developed into a "nuptial Mass" and, finally, into a full marriage rite which, by the twelfth century, was under the supervision of the clergy and was taking place at the front door of the church.[3] By the time of the Reformation, the entire marriage service had entered the church building itself. Though the Reformers made many modifications in other areas of worship, they left the marriage rites almost unchanged. They translated them into the language of the people and simplified them somewhat, but found major alterations unnecessary.[4]

In recent times the church has begun to reexamine the theological purposes and language of its marriage rites. Some elements of the older English-language services (e.g., the words, which are found in some rites, "to have and to hold, from this day forward . . . ," and the action of "giving away" the bride) speak more of a property contract than of a steadfast covenant between two people. Some of the newer, "experimental" marriage rites have proved to be less than satisfactory linguistically and theologically. This resource, which attempts to present contemporary marriage rites firmly grounded in the theological convictions of the Reformed heritage, has been prepared for the Presbyterian Church (U.S.A.) and the Cumberland Presbyterian Church. Many similar revisions of the marriage rite have been sponsored by other denominations and have been published over the last decade.

Theological Convictions

Christian theologians have tended to view marriage from two important perspectives. First, marriage is understood to be grounded in the doctrine of creation and thus the gift of God to all humanity. From this perspective, marriage is not the exclusive possession of the Christian faith; it belongs to the whole of human society. Just as Christians rejoice when the civil government justly rules, they also rejoice when marriage is honored and wisely administered in the public realm. From this perspective, Christians marry by "the authority of the state," participating in the same social reality as all others who marry.

Christians, however, also view marriage as an issue of discipleship. They understand marriage to be grounded in the doctrine of redemption as well as in creation. They seek to bring their marriages into accord with the will of God and to allow their relationship with Christ to form the pattern for the covenant of marriage (Eph. 5:21ff.). In Baptism, Christians are called to a life of service in the name of Christ, and marriage is one of the places where that mission can be expressed. Marriage for a Christian is not disjointed from marriage as a general social reality, but it takes on a special character because it is governed by a commitment to Christ. The promises of marriage are connected to the promises of Baptism, and it is therefore fitting that these promises be made in the context of worship and be witnessed by the community of faith.

The rites presented in this resource are services of Christian worship. They express praise and thanksgiving to God for the gift of marriage, and they embody the trinitarian faith of the Christian community. They assume that at least one of the marriage partners is a faithful member of the Christian community. Moreover, they assume that the promises of marriage are to be made in response to the Word of God, in the context of prayer, and in the presence of the community of faith.

Freedom and Form

The marriage rites in this resource are attempts to preserve a healthy balance between liturgical form, tradition, and order, on the one hand, and liturgical freedom and flexibility, on the other. Because weddings are particularly subject to being misunderstood as private and family events rather than as services of corporate worship, it is especially important that marriage rites be expressions of the church's liturgical life and understanding, and not merely the private and personal statements of the couple. Ministers may wish to invite the couple to help compose certain elements in the service, but the popular idea that the couple can "write their own wedding" contains the mistaken notion that the service belongs only to the bride and groom. The marriage rite is public worship, and it includes affirmations about the nature of worship and marriage that transcend the concerns of any one wedding. A marriage rite that contained only the words and thoughts of the couple would, in most cases, be far too narrow and therefore less than the bride and groom deserve. The wedding includes claims and promises, prayers and blessings, which together speak of a vision of marriage broader, deeper, and more helpful than any of us can see apart from the witness of the larger church.

These rites contain, therefore, much that is traditional in language, theological claim, and order, but there is also room for flexibility and adaptation. Authentic worship is "in the Spirit," and the Spirit's action cannot be expressed by any single liturgical pattern. Free prayer, a different sequence of elements, or careful changes in the language of the service are all appropriate in certain circumstances. Moreover, weddings, even though they do not "belong" solely to the bride and groom, should reflect the couple's ethnic, cultural, and personal situation. Certain flexibilities are built into the rites themselves. Options are given for alternate orders of worship, declarations of intent, vows, and prayers. The choices regarding music and Scripture provide other opportunities for adapting the service to particular needs and settings.

Scripture

Since the marriage rites included here are understood to be services of worship, Scripture is given a prominent place in each of them. Christian marriage is a response to the Word of God and is governed by that Word. This is expressed in the rites not only by the fact that Scripture lessons are read in the service but also by the large number of biblical phrases and allusions found throughout the services.

There are several passages in the Bible that speak directly about marriage, and there are some other passages that employ marriage as a metaphor for the nature of the Kingdom of God (e.g., the "wedding" parables, Revelation 19). The biblical witness regarding marriage is not confined, however, to these texts. Any passage that speaks about one of the prominent theological themes of marriage (e.g., creation, covenant, blessing, discipleship) illumines the nature of Christian marriage. A selection of Scripture readings that have traditionally been employed at weddings is included on pages 69–77 of this resource, but many other passages are also suitable.

Since preaching is a primary means by which God's Word is made present for the community of faith, it is strongly recommended that every service of marriage include a brief sermon.

Marriage and the Sacraments

Although marriage is not itself viewed as a sacrament in the Reformed theological tradition, it is firmly connected to both of the sacraments, Baptism and the Lord's Supper.

In Baptism, Christians are given a new identity and called to a special way of life. For Christians who marry, marriage is one of the places where this baptismal identification with Christ is seen and the calling to work for the cause of Christ is expressed. The oneness between husband and wife and the steadfast promises they make to each other, represented in the wedding, point to the unity and covenant love between Christ and the church, which is seen in Baptism (Eph. 5:32).

The Lord's Supper is the sacrament of Christ's continual presence, feeding, and sustaining of the people of God for mission. At the Lord's table, Christians are called to serve Christ by serving each other and the world, a call that encompasses every relationship, including marriage. Christ is present in the Lord's Supper, and the promises of marriage cannot be kept nor the responsibilities of marriage fulfilled without Christ's continual and strengthening presence.

It is sometimes quite fitting for the marriage service itself to include a celebration of the Lord's Supper. Indeed, gathering at the Lord's table with the bride and groom was one of the first ways in which the ancient church connected marriage to worship. Special care should be exercised, however, in deciding whether to include the Lord's Supper in the wedding, and some guidelines for this decision are included on page 98.

People and Participation

The temptation for the congregation to assume a "spectator mentality," which is a threat to worship generally, is particularly strong at weddings. All of these rites are built upon the conviction that the witnesses to the marriage promises are far more than just "invited guests" at the wedding. Each of the rites begins with a call to worship, and many opportunities are given for the congregation to respond to that call with active participation in the worship. Congregational singing is encouraged. Corporate prayers and responses are included. The whole congregation is asked to make a vocal promise to do everything in its power to uphold the couple in their marriage. The congregation may be invited to join the minister in saying, "Those whom God has joined together, let no one separate." Some of these responses can be given "by heart." On other occasions, copies of the marriage rite, hymnals, bulletins, or other printed resources can be provided for the congregation as aids to their participation.

It is important to note that the marriage liturgy serves not only the couple in their marriage but also all others who are present. The service provides opportunities for all to remember promises they have made and to recommit themselves to those promises. As vows are spoken, married couples can renew their own vows. The statements about marriage, the lessons from Scripture, and the prayers remind the congregation of their mission to all families and challenge the people to exercise their responsibilities for mutual support and care.

The Language of the Rites

Care has been taken in the development of these rites to select for each of the components wording that would embody the best available liturgical language. The editors sought to discover phrasing that would be contemporary, but not trendy; clear, but also poetically sensitive. Attention was given to the fact that the words of these services would be spoken aloud. Therefore, as an aid to the minister and the other participants, the rites are presented on the printed page in short phrases, each designed to be spoken as a unit.

Some of the language of these services was written for this resource and thus is new. Most of it, however, has been gleaned (and, in some cases adapted) from previous Presbyterian and Reformed marriage rites, from the Bible, and from the rich ecumenical liturgical heritage. Several denominations, including the Lutheran and Episcopal churches, have recently produced contemporary marriage services. Their rites have been invaluable to the editors in the choice of language.

As is the case with all of the resources in this series, care was taken in regard to the use of inclusive language. The same guidelines specified in *The Service for the Lord's Day* (Supplemental Liturgical Resource 1) were followed in these rites.[5] The suggested Scripture readings contained in this resource are all from the Revised Standard Version of the Bible, without alteration. Changes in the language of the lessons are left to the discretion of those using this resource.

2

THE THREE MARRIAGE RITES:
GUIDELINES FOR USE

Selecting the Appropriate Rite

There are three services for Christian marriage in this resource, and each service is designed for use when certain circumstances prevail.

Rite I—A Service for General Use is a brief service that is suitable for use in almost every setting. All three rites provide many suggestions for vocal participation by the congregation, but since this service can, if necessary, be conducted without hymnbooks, bulletins, or any other printed resources, it can be used in the regular worship space, in a home, out-of-doors, or in other locations. Persons familiar with the "traditional" marriage services (such as the ones in *The Book of Common Worship* or *The Worshipbook*) will find this rite to be different in language, but similar in structure, length, and application.

Rite II—A Service Based Upon the Service for the Lord's Day contains an ordering of elements that is very much like that found in the classical pattern of Sunday worship (gathering, call to worship, praise, confession, etc.). It can be used when the wedding is to be incorporated into the regular Lord's Day worship or on any other day when the full pattern of Christian worship is desired. The service includes the option of celebrating the Lord's Supper.

Rite III—A Service Recognizing a Civil Marriage is to be used on those occasions when a couple, having been previously married in a civil ceremony, now wish to have their marriage promises witnessed by the community of faith. Except for a few changes in language, made to conform to the fact that the couple are already legally married, this service is the same as Rite I.

The decision of which rite to use is the responsibility of the minister, but in most cases this choice can best be made in consultation with the couple.

Preparing for the Wedding

Preparations for the wedding should be made in at least the following four areas:

1. Session Approval. In Presbyterian government, the session has responsibility for supervising the worship life of the congregation. Since weddings are services of worship, the session should exercise general oversight in this area. While it is usually desirable to delegate to the minister most of the responsibility for the specific planning of each wedding, many sessions have found it useful to develop general guidelines for weddings, including policies on such matters as music, flowers and other decorations, photography during the service, fees, and other matters.

2. Legal Requirements. The laws regarding marriage vary from state to state. In the conduct of weddings, ministers function primarily as representatives of the church, but they also bear responsibilities to the state. Ministers should become familiar with the legal requirements in their geographical areas and be careful to ensure that these provisions are satisfied in every case.

3. Pastoral Care. Before the wedding, ministers will want to meet with the couple to provide pastoral care for them at this important time in their lives. Part of this care should be devoted to reviewing the marriage service itself, and suggestions for doing this are included on page 101.

The pastoral relationship developed with the couple does not end, of course, at the time of the wedding. Many ministers have found it helpful to spend time with the couple during the first few weeeks of their marriage, to make a pastoral visit on the occasion of the first anniversary of their wedding, or even to provide a special program of education, counseling, and support for the newly married.

4. The Rehearsal. If possible, the couple and the other members of the wedding party should be given an opportunity to rehearse their responsibilities for the service. Not only does this prepare and reassure the participants, it also gives the minister an occasion to interpret, for the full wedding party, the character of the marriage service as worship.

Conducting the Rites

Rite I—A Service for General Use

Entrance

The purpose of the entrance is simply to bring the bride, groom, and other members of the wedding party to a position in front of the minister and in view of the congregation, who will witness the marriage promises. The custom of the bride and her attendants processing to the front of the church is often followed, but it is by no means required. The bride and the groom may process together, the wedding party may simply gather at the appointed time in front of the minister, the parents of the bride may accompany the bride and the parents of the groom may accompany the groom in the procession, or another practice suitable to the particular circumstances may be used. The congregation may be invited to stand as the wedding party enters. Whatever procedure is followed, care should be taken to symbolize the equal importance of both bride and groom and of the two families from which they come.

The following placements of the wedding party can serve as guides:

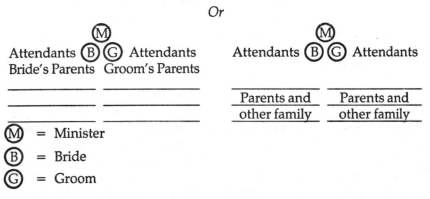

If music is used during the entrance, it should be chosen on the basis of its suitability for a service of worship. Specific guidelines and resources for the selection of music can be found on pages 100, 103–111.

Sentences of Scripture

Because the wedding is a service of worship, it begins with sentences of Scripture, which serve as a call to worship. Two selections are given in the rite. The verse from 1 John announces that God is the source of all human love, and Ps. 118:24 calls for joy in response to the creative activity of God. Each emphasizes an important theological theme related to marriage.

Statement on the Gift of Marriage

These words, spoken by the minister, serve three purposes. First, they remind the congregation of why they have gathered. Second, they provide a summary of what the church understands about marriage biblically and theologically by announcing the promises and actions of God in regard to marriage. And third, they provide ethical instruction regarding the responsibilities of marriage, not only for the bride and groom but also for the whole congregation.

"We have gathered . . ." The opening paragraph reminds the congregation that they are not passive spectators at the wedding. Theirs is to be an active role. They are to worship God, in particular, giving thanks for the gift of marriage. They are called to pray for the couple that their life together will be a place of strength and that their marriage will nourish not only their love for each other but also their love for God. No marriage covenant can be sustained in isolation, and the congregation is called to express the support of the community of faith by witnessing the promises that will be made this day.

"God created us male and female . . ." Biblically, marriage has its origins in God's creation of human beings as male and female, to provide for them steadfast companionship and mutual support (Gen. 2:18–25; Mark 10:7–8).

"God gave us marriage for the full expression of the love between a man and a woman . . ." This is the first of three statements that begin with the refrain, "God gave us . . ." Marriage, which from a sociological perspective is a product of human society, is also understood theologically to be a good and gracious gift of God. A wedding is the only service of worship in the life of the church where sexuality and sexual union are major themes, and the phrase "the full expression of the love between a man and a woman" acknowledges that fact. In the lifelong covenant of marriage, the sexual relationship between a man and a woman finds its richest physical, emotional, and spiritual expression. "They are no longer two but one flesh" (Mark 10:8). The statement "In marriage a woman and a man belong to each other" further points to the depth of the marriage covenant and echoes the word of Paul in 1 Cor. 7:3–7 regarding the sexual mutuality of marriage.

"God gave us marriage . . . for the birth and nurture of children . . ." This statement affirms the role of marriage in sustaining humankind and the place of marriage as a basic unit of ordered human society. The birth and nurture of children are essential for the continuation of the human race and are an expression of hope and confidence in God's providential care. Since this statement is part of a general declaration about the church's understanding of marriage, it is ordinarily appropriate to say these words even if the particular couple being married, for reasons of health, age, or personal choice, are unlikely to have children themselves. At this point in the service, the theological affirmations are about marriage in general. Later in the rite the language will become more focused upon the specific marriage being celebrated this day.

"God gave us marriage as a holy mystery . . ." This statement is based upon Eph. 5:31–33, in which the relationship between a husband and a wife is presented as a profound mystery, analogous to the relationship between Christ and the church. Marriage, therefore, points beyond itself to the redemptive activity of God in Christ.

"In marriage, husband and wife are called to a new way of life . . ." Here the church affirms that the choice to marry is, in a sense, a vocational choice. In Baptism all Christians are called to a new way of life, and Christians who are married are to express that baptismal call in and through their marriages. Marriage is not a place where two self-serving people meet to satisfy their desires; it is a journey of faith where two are joined as one in Christ for discipleship and mission

"We rejoice . . ." The closing statement is a trinitarian affirmation of the presence and blessing of God in marriage and a call to the community to respond by upholding the honor of marriage (Heb. 13:4). An alternate text of the Statement on the Gift of Marriage is provided on page 61.

Prayer

This brief prayer rejoices that God is faithful in keeping promises, and seeks the presence of the Holy Spirit for the couple as they make their promises. Marriage vows are radical promises, promises that cannot be kept relying upon human resources alone. This prayer asks for the sustaining and strengthening power of God's Spirit. An alternate text of this prayer is provided on page 63.

Declarations of Intent

This element replaces the "betrothal vows" found in many traditional services of marriage. The church has declared, in the statement on the gift of marriage, its convictions about marriage, and now, in the light of this understanding, the man and the woman are asked if they wish to be married. By responding, "I do," the bride and groom indicate that they come as free, discerning, and willing partners to the covenant of marriage.

Two choices for the declaration of intent are given. One specifically connects marriage to Baptism and thus assumes that both bride and groom are baptized. The other does not make the baptismal connection explicit and, while it is suitable for any wedding, it should always be chosen when one of the marriage partners is not baptized. The same declaration should be used for both the man and the woman.

It has often been the practice, both here and at the point of the marriage vows, to address the man first and then the woman. This order is no doubt shaped by custom and cultural considerations, and there is no theological or liturgical basis for it. Some may wish to use one ordering for the declaration of intent and then reverse the sequence for the marriage vows.

Affirmations of the Families

This element provides opportunity for the families of the bride and groom to express their love for the couple, to offer their blessing to them, and to pledge their support for the marriage. The affirmations of the families emphasize not only the willingness of the families to bless the couple but also their readiness to release them into this new relationship. There are no provisions in this service for "giving the bride away," an outdated practice based upon the concept of the transfer of property from one owner to another.

In many weddings, this affirmation will be given, in turn, by the parents of the bride and groom. They may already be standing with the wedding party in front of the congregation (if they have participated in the procession), or, if they are seated in the congregation, they may be asked to stand at this point in the service. The minister addresses them in a way deemed appropriate: "John and Mary, do you give . . . ," or "Do you, the parents of Susan, give . . . ," or "Do you, the members of the Smith family, give . . . ," or other similar words. Two responses, one longer, the other briefer, are provided as alternatives. It is preferable that both families, if present, give affirmations. Following the affirmations, the families may, if desired, be seated among the congregation.

Affirmation of the Congregation

Marriage is more than a private relationship between a man and a woman, and it is not just a matter between two families. Marriage is the concern of the whole community, and a marriage depends upon the support of the community. In this element, the congregation is given the opportunity to voice this community support and to pledge continuing responsibility toward the marriage. The congregation may remain seated, or may be asked to stand.

Scripture and Sermon

Christians seek in their marriages, as well as in the rest of life, to be obedient to the Word of God. At this point in the service, God's Word is expressed through the reading of Scripture. Several Scripture lessons that are particularly suitable for weddings have been included (pp. 69–77), but many other texts that refer to the praise of God, the love of Christ, the calling of Christians, or the disciplines of the Christian life are also fitting.

The reading of Scripture may be preceded by the singing of a psalm, hymn, spiritual, or anthem, and by a prayer for illumination. One or two readings are usually sufficient, and they do not have to be read by the minister. Members of the family, the wedding party, or other members of the congregation may be asked to serve as readers. The Scripture readings may be followed by a brief sermon. The sermon should be based upon one or more of the readings, and, while acknowledging the special circumstances of the day and the needs of the bride, the groom, and their families, it should be addressed to the whole congregation.

Vows

The essence of the marriage rite is the making of promises. The man and the woman make public promises to each other in the context of promises made by their families, promises made by the congregation, and, most important, promises made by God. The promises contained in the marriage vows are phrased in the present tense, but they are oriented toward the future. They are therefore expressions of hope as well as of faith and love.

Because the marriage of a man and a woman is a sign of the covenant relationship between Christ and the church, the promises made in marriage are expressed in unequivocal language. The man and the woman pledge themselves to each other not for as long as it is convenient, but for "as long as we both shall live." This unwavering and lifelong commitment is a sign both of God's steadfast covenant and of the high responsibilities of marriage. Many marriages of course do not endure. Moreover, human sinfulness mars every relationship, even those marriages which do last for a lifetime, and no marriage perfectly embodies the marriage promises to be loving and faithful in all circumstances. Yet we are bold to make these promises because we do not make them in our own strength alone. We believe that God is present and active in the covenant of marriage. In marriage, human beings seek to keep the radical promises they have made to each other, knowing that in many ways they will fail, in the faith that their efforts will be strengthened by God and that, by the grace of God, their actions, even the failures, will point to the faithfulness of God, who never fails.

Every effort should be made to make visible as well as vocal the centrality of the making of promises. The minister is not "performing their marriage"; they are marrying each other by their promises. The minister and the couple may even move to another location (e.g., up into the chancel area) in order to give visual emphasis to this portion of the service.

The bride and the groom turn to face each other, joining their right hands as they speak their vows. Either of two customs may be followed here. The couple may join their right hands, keeping them joined through both vows. A second possibility is for the one saying the vow to take the right hand of the other, releasing the hand after the vow is spoken.

During the rehearsal, the couple should be encouraged to speak their vows clearly and loudly enough to be heard by those witnessing the marriage. It is the custom in some places for the congregation to stand during the speaking of the vows.

Even though the text of the rite preserves the traditional custom of presenting the man's vow first, the minister may, as noted above, wish to employ one order for the declarations of intent and the reverse order for the vows.

The usual custom is for the minister to speak small sections of the vows and for the couple, in turn, to repeat the words spoken by the minister. This is to be preferred over the practice of the couple memorizing and "reciting" the vows, not only for practical reasons but also because it emphasizes that the vows themselves are part of the church's liturgical heritage. The church, which has through the centuries sought prayerfully to discern God's will for marriage, now provides for this couple, as they make their promises on their special day, its most thoughtful language.

Two choices are given for the vows. It is important that the same form of the vow be used for both the bride and the groom

Exchange of Rings (or Other Symbols)

The exchanging of rings, or other symbols, serves as a visible and tangible confirmation of the marriage promises. Since the exchanging of gifts simply underscores the promise-making which has already taken place, it is an optional element in the service.

Many American Presbyterians are most familiar with the use of rings as the symbols that are exchanged. In some geographical locations and in some ethnic traditions other symbols, such as coins or food, are employed. With minor changes in language, this element can be adapted to embrace these other symbols.

The minister addresses the couple, saying, "What do you bring as the sign of your promise?" At this point the rings are brought forth, and the ring blessing may be said by the minister. The minister may want to hold both of the rings, or the bride and groom may hold them. It should be noted that the focus of the ring blessing is not on the rings themselves but on the relationship between the man and the woman signified by the rings.

Two possible texts are presented in the rite. The first involves a statement by the one giving the ring, followed by a response from the one receiving the ring. The second text does not have a response.

It is important to observe that both texts end with the traditional trinitarian formula, "in the name of the Father, and of the Son, and of the Holy Spirit." When one of the marriage partners is not a Christian, this formula should be omitted for *both* bride and groom. In the statement on the gift of marriage, the trinitarian grounding of the church's understanding of marriage has already been affirmed. While being clear about its own commitments, the church does not ask people to make personal confessions of faith which are not honest. When a Christian marries a person who is not a part of the Christian community, the trinitarian language at this point in the service becomes inappropriate. The formula is omitted for both bride and groom in order to express the equality of the covenant being made.

Prayer

After the marriage promises have been made (and, if desired, confirmed by the exchange of gifts), prayers are offered, asking that the couple be given the grace to fulfill their mutual vows, that all marriages be strengthened, and that the couple along with the whole congregation be equipped for mission in the world.

Two prayer texts are provided as alternatives. Since the prayer after the marriage promises should make specific petitions on behalf of the couple and the other worshipers, it is also fitting for free prayer to be used here, either replacing the prayers given in the rite or being incorporated into them. It should be noted that the first prayer option includes a section, enclosed in brackets, regarding the gift of children. In some situations, because of the age or health of the couple, or because of other pastoral considerations, this section of the prayer should be omitted. Additional alternative texts for this prayer are provided on pages 63–65.

The Lord's Prayer may be sung or said. It is better for the whole congregation to pray it in unison than for the prayer to be sung by a soloist or a choir. Prayers sung by soloists or choirs can, of course, be understood as prayers offered on behalf of all of the worshipers. The Lord's Prayer, however, is a widely known prayer, and its use provides a significant opportunity for congregational participation, so often lacking in a service of marriage.

Announcement of Marriage

The minister announces to the congregation that the man and the woman are married by virtue of the vows they have made to each other. The minister enables this to be symbolized by joining the right hands of the couple. One custom that can make this even more dramatic is for the minister to wrap their hands with his or her stole, visually emphasizing the bond now formed between them.

The words, "Those whom God has joined together let no one separate," based on Mark 10:9, are said either by the minister or by the minister and the congregation.

Charge to the Couple

Here the minister charges the couple, using words of Scripture to remind them of the ethical responsibilities of marriage. Two texts, both based upon the language of Colossians 3, are given as alternatives. The reference to crowning in the first option has a rich symbolic association with marriage. There is an ancient practice of crowning the couple in the marriage liturgy of the Eastern Church.

Benediction

The benediction is intended both for the couple and for the congregation. Two textual options are given. The first is an adaptation of the traditional Aaronic blessing from Num. 6:24–26. The second is built upon a trinitarian structure.

The benediction marks the conclusion of the service. The wedding party may wish simply to leave along with the other members of the congregation, or they may recess as music is played or sung.

Rite II—A Service Based Upon the Service for the Lord's Day

This rite is based upon the order of service found in *The Service for the Lord's Day* (Supplemental Liturgical Resource 1). It is envisioned that this rite may serve as a wedding service, per se, or as a regular Sunday service that includes a service of marriage. The components of this service therefore have been selected with the general purpose of worship in mind, though most of them emphasize theological themes integral to marriage. For example:

1. The alternative texts for the call to worship emphasize the themes of joy and love.

2. The call to confession, from Jeremiah 31, and the prayer for illumination present the covenant image.

3. One of the alternative texts for the prayer of confession acknowledges that "we have broken the promises we have made to you and to one another."

4. The great prayer of thanksgiving (to be used when the Lord's Supper is included) and the prayer of thanksgiving (to be used when the Lord's Supper is omitted) praise God for the gift of marriage.

5. The prayer after the Lord's Supper employs the biblical imagery of the marriage feast.

Following the sermon (and, if desired, a creed and a congregational song), the bride, groom, and other members of the wedding party present themselves in front of the minister and in view of the congregation, who will witness the marriage promises. This should be done as simply as possible. In many instances, the members of the wedding party will come from the congregation to their positions during the singing of a hymn.

The service proceeds in the same manner as Rite I through the charge to the couple. At this point there are several options for completing the service:

1. The service may continue following the Lord's Day pattern including the Lord's Supper. The blessing for the couple is followed by prayers of intercession, the offering, preparation of the table, the invitation to the Lord's table, the great prayer of thanksgiving, the breaking of the bread, the communion of the people, the prayer

after Communion, congregational singing, a charge, and a general blessing.

The text of a great prayer of thanksgiving which was composed specifically for this resource is included. Other texts may be found in *The Service for the Lord's Day* (Supplemental Liturgical Resource 1). (See especially Prayer A with Christian Marriage I or II variations.)

When the Lord's Supper is observed at a wedding, care should be taken to avoid any hint of a "private ceremony." The Lord's table is open to all baptized Christians, and there is no theological justification for the practice of only the couple partaking of the sacrament. The invitation to the table should be issued to the whole congregation. Since the Lord's Supper involves the active participation of the Christian community, services of marriage in which only the family, or some other small and select group, are present do not usually provide suitable settings for the observance of the sacrament.

The Lord's Supper should be observed only in the context of a full service of worship, including the preaching of the Word. The observance of the Lord's Supper should be approved by the session, and at least one member of the session should be present.

Weddings are services of worship, but in our culture they are also public events, and the guests at a wedding may include many people who are not members of the Christian community and Christians who are not comfortable receiving Communion in traditions other than their own. In such circumstances, the celebration of the Lord's Supper may be awkward or unnecessarily divisive. Pastoral judgment should be exercised in regard to the wisdom of including the sacrament as a part of the marriage rite.

2. The service may continue along the pattern of a Lord's Day service that does not include the Lord's Supper. The blessing for the couple is followed by prayers of intercession, the offering, a prayer of thanksgiving, congregational singing, a charge, and a general blessing.

3. The service may conclude here. A blessing is addressed specifically to the couple, and after optional music, the service concludes with a general blessing. The wedding party may recess after the general blessing.

Rite III—A Service Recognizing a Civil Marriage

This rite, designed for use when the couple have been married in a civil ceremony, is almost identical to Rite I, and it can be conducted following the suggestions given for that rite. The following changes have been made in the language of Rite I to reflect the fact that the couple are already married:

1. The statement of marriage indicates that the couple "are married according to the law of the state."

2. The couple are called "in faith" to make their promises to each other "as husband and wife."

3. The vows state, "You are my wife (husband)."

3

MUSIC AND THE WEDDING

The marriage rite is a service of worship, and the music that is selected for the wedding should embody the same high standards applied to the music chosen for worship generally. Wedding music should focus upon God and emphasize the faith of the Christian community rather than romantic love or sentimentality.

The minister has the final authority for the ordering of worship and the selection of music to be used. The minister will want to consult with the church musicians and others with musical expertise regarding the best available music for use in the marriage rite. Musical standards and aesthetic judgment are subjective, but the trained musician can be helpful regarding standards of musical excellence and theological integrity. Ordinarily, musicians on the church staff are granted the privilege of playing for the marriage service, but they may defer to a guest musician if they choose.

Suggestions of musical selections that are suitable at various places in the marriage rite are included in this resource on pp. 103–111. The lists are, of course, not complete; many other compositions are also appropriate for weddings.

4

THE WEDDING RITE AND PASTORAL CARE

People shape liturgics, and then liturgies shape people. The liturgy is not only the instrument for our worship, it also teaches. Most ministers will want to include, as a part of their program of premarital counseling, a review of the marriage rite itself. This can be the occasion not only when couples help to shape the marriage service but also when the minister can do some teaching about the church's convictions concerning marriage. Because the marriage rite expresses, in liturgical language, the basic theological affirmation of the church in regard to marriage, it is a good instrument for that education process. In similar fashion, the marriage liturgy can be used as a study resource for adult education in the church.

A copy of the marriage rite may be given to the couple after the service. As they read and remember the service, they are afforded the opportunity to renew their promises.

Many couples who come to be married will have been previously married, and then divorced. The high view of marriage and the permanence of the vows expressed in the marriage rite will provide the occasion for conversation about the love and forgiveness of Christ. No one is fully able to keep the marriage vows, and every married person depends upon the grace of Christ, who is faithful even when we are not, to sustain the covenant of marriage.

NOTES

1. There is some evidence that the early Christian community did depart from the Roman legal custom in one important area. Christians who were slaves were sometimes considered by the church to be married "in the Lord," even though they were prohibited from marrying, in a legal sense, by Roman statute.

2. James F. White, *Introduction to Christian Worship* (Abingdon Press, 1980), p. 239.

3. Ibid., p. 240.

4. Ibid., p. 241.

5. *The Service for the Lord's Day* (Supplemental Liturgical Resource 1) (Westminster Press, 1984), p. 146. The paper, "Inclusive Language–Definition and Guidelines," adopted by the 197th General Assembly (1985) of the Presbyterian Church (U.S.A.), also guided the task force.

MUSIC FOR THE WEDDING

Following is a list of music appropriate for the wedding service. A more extensive list, which is available from the Office of Worship of the Presbyterian Church (U.S.A.), 1044 Alta Vista Road, Louisville, KY 40205, includes further suggestions for the categories below as well as suggestions for organ with instruments, instruments without organ, handbells, and choral music.

Key:

[E]   Easy
[M]   Moderately difficult
[D]   Difficult

A. Instrumental Music Appropriate for Pre-Service Music

Bach, J. S.
  Prelude and Fugues (Kalmus) [ED]
  Chorale Prelude, "Rejoice, Beloved Christians" (Kalmus) [D]
  Fugue in G Major—"Gigue" (Kalmus) [D]
Brahms, Johannes
  Chorale Prelude, "Deck Thyself, My Soul, with Gladness" (Marks) [M]
Buxtehude, Dietrich
  Chorale Prelude, "Now Pray We to the Holy Spirit" (Hedar) [E]
Handel, G. F.
  Organ Concerti (A-R Edition)

Haydn, F. J.
  The Musical Clocks (H. W. Gray) [E]
Mendelssohn, Felix
  Organ Sonatas (G. Henle Verlag)
Vaughan Williams, Ralph
  Prelude on "Rhosymedre" (Stainer and Bell) [M]

Collections
The Parish Organist, Wedding Music, Part IX, ed. Thomas Gieschen
  (Concordia) [EM]
Wedding Music, Part II, General Service Music (Concordia) [EM]

> *Collections such as the following are particularly useful for pianos or
> small organs with manuals only:*

Bach, J. S. *Chorales* (Associated, G. Schirmer, Peters) [E]
Biggs, E. Power. *Manuals Only* (Associated) [EM]
Franck, César. *L'Organiste*, Vols. 1 and 2 (Enoch) [E]
Handel, G. F. *Twelve Voluntaries* (Concordia) [EM]
Johnson, David N. *Manuals Only* (Augsburg) [EM]
Langlais, Jean. *24 Pieces for Harmonium or Organ* (Philippo) [M]
McAfee, Don. *Early English Keyboard Music*, Vols. 1 and 2 (McAfee
  Music Co.) [EM]
Peeters, Flor
  Heures Intimes, Vols. 1 and 2 (Leomine) [EM]
  Thirty-five Miniatures for Organ (McLaughlin and Reilly) [M]
Telemann, Georg Philipp. *12 Easy Chorale Preludes* (Peters) [E]
Vierne, Louis. *24 Pièces en Style Libre*, Vols. 1 and 2 (Durand) [MD]
Eight Short Pieces for Manuals Only (Oxford) [EM]
Eighty Choral Preludes of the 17th and 18th Centuries (Peters) [M]

B. Instrumental Processional (Entrance)
and Recessional

Bach, J. S.
  "Concerto in A Minor," Movement 1 (G. Schirmer) [D]
  "Grave" from *Fantasia in G Major* (Kalmus) [M]
Boyce, William
  "Trumpet Tune in D" (Oxford) [M]

Brahms, Johannes
"St. Anthony Chorale" from *Variations on a Theme by Haydn* (Brodt) [E]
Busarow, Donald
Processional on "Lift High the Cross" (Concordia) [M]
Campra, André
"Rigaudon" (H. W. Gray) [E]
Gigout, Eugène
"Grand Choeur Dialogue" (Durand) [D]
Greene, Maurice
"A Trumpet Tune" (Cramer) [E]
Handel, G. F.
Suite from Water Music: "Allegro vivace," "Allegro maestoso," "Hornpipe" (J. Fischer) [EM]
Hillert, Richard
"Processional Music for Manuals Alone" (Concordia) [E]
Johnson, David N.
"Three Trumpet Tunes for Organ" (Augsburg) [M]
"Trumpet Tune in D Major" (Augsburg) [M]
Marcello, Benedetto
"Psalm XIX" (H. W. Gray) [EM]
Mendelssohn, Felix
"Allegro maestoso e vivace" from *Sonata II* (Hannsler Verlag) [M]
Mouret, Jean Joseph
"Rondeau" from *Sinfonies de Fanfares* (H. W. Gray) [M]
Near, Gerald
"A Wedding Processional" (H. W. Gray) [M]
Purcell, Henry
"Trumpet Tune in D Major," in *Wedding Music, Part I* (Concordia) [E]
"Trumpet Voluntary in D Major" (also known as "Prince of Denmark March" by Jeremiah Clarke), in *Wedding Music, Part I* (Concordia) [E]
Shaw, Martin
"Wedding Processional" (H. W. Gray) [M]
Stanley, John
"Trumpet Voluntary" from *Suite for Organ* (Oxford) [M]
Widor, Charles Marie
"Toccata" from *Fifth Symphony* (Marks) [D]

Collections
Wedding Music, Part I: Processionals, Recessionals (Concordia) [EM]
Wedding Music, Book II, ed. David N. Johnson. Processionals and
   Recessionals (Augsburg) [EM]

C. Hymns

Many of the hymns listed below are appropriate for use in other
sections of the service than the section for which they are listed, and
therefore are interchangeable.

HL   *The Hymnal*
HB   *The Hymnbook*
WB   *The Worshipbook*

1. *Hymns Appropriate for Processional (Entrance)*
or Recessional

	HL	HB	WB
Joyful, Joyful, We Adore Thee	5	21	446
Now Thank We All Our God	459	9	481
Praise, My Soul, the King of Heaven	14	31	551
Praise to the Lord, the Almighty	6	1	557

2. *Hymns Appropriate for Praise*

	HL	HB	WB
For the Beauty of the Earth	71	2	372
Let Us with a Gladsome Mind	64	28	453
O Come and Sing Unto the Lord	49	29	488
O Lord, Our Lord, in All the Earth	—	95	515
O Worship the King All Glorious Above	2	26	533
Praise the Lord, His Glories Show	12	4	552
Praise the Lord, Who Reigns Above	—	—	553

3. *Hymns Appropriate to Follow*
the Declarations of Intent and Vows

	HL	HB	WB
Be Thou My Vision	325	303	304
Blessed Jesus, at Your Word	—	—	309
God of Our Life, Through All the Circling Years	88	108	395
God of the Ages, by Whose Hand	—	—	396
If Thou but Suffer God to Guide Thee	105	344	431

4. Hymns Appropriate to Follow the Creed
or Presentation of Wedding Party

	HL	HB	WB
Call Jehovah Thy Salvation	292	123	322
Come Down, O Love Divine	—	—	334
Come, Holy Spirit, God and Lord!	—	—	336
Love Divine, All Loves Excelling	308	399	471
O Perfect Love	484	453	—
Spirit Divine, Attend Our Prayers	212	243	574

5. Hymns Particularly Appropriate
When the Wedding Includes the Lord's Supper

	HL	HB	WB
A Hymn of Glory Let Us Sing	—	—	273
At the Name of Jesus	—	143	303
Become to Us the Living Bread	—	—	305
Be Known to Us in Breaking Bread	356	446	—
Bread of Heaven, on Thee We Feed	—	—	313
Come, Risen Lord, and Deign to Be Our Guest	—	—	340
Deck Yourself, My Soul, with Gladness	—	—	351
Father, We Greet You	—	285	364
Jesus, Thou Joy of Loving Hearts	354	215	510
We Greet You, Sure Redeemer from All Strife	—	—	625
Where Charity and Love Prevail	—	—	641

D. Music from Black, Hispanic, and Asian American Sources

CLS   *Celebremos* (Nashville: Discipleship Resources, 1983)

HFW   *Hymns from the Four Winds* (Supplemental Worship Resources 13) (Abingdon Press, 1983)

SZ   *Songs of Zion* (Supplemental Worship Resources 12) (Abingdon Press, 1981)

WB   *The Worshipbook* (Westminster Press, 1972)

Come, O Gracious King (Asian)	HFW	113
Here, O Lord, Your Servants Gather (Asian)	WB	417
I Lift Up My Eyes to the Mountains (Ps. 121) (Asian)	HFW	117
In God We Trust (Black)	SZ	214
Let Us Break Bread Together (Black)	WB	452
Lord God, Long Before Creation (Asian)	HFW	12
Más y Más (More and More) (Hispanic)	CLS	44

May the Lord, Mighty God (Asian)	*HFW*	118
O Give Thanks to the Lord (Ps. 136) (Asian)	*HFW*	120
Peace Unto You (Black)	*SZ*	223
Prayer for Families (Black)	*SZ*	9
Tú Estás Presente (You Are Here Beside Us) (Hispanic)	*CLS*	43

E. Musical Settings of Psalms Appropriate to the Marriage Rite

Resources cited below, in addition to the hymnals, are:

The Gelineau Gradual (G.I.A. Publications, Inc., 1969, 1975, 1977). A collection of responsorial psalms from The Grail/Gelineau Psalter. Order from G.I.A. Publications, Inc., 7404 S. Mason Avenue, Chicago, IL 60638. Order no. G-2124.

Music from Taizé, by Jacques Berthier. Order from G.I.A. Publications, Inc., 7404 S. Mason Avenue, Chicago, IL 60638. Order no. G-2433.

A Psalm Sampler (Westminster Press, 1986). Developed by the Office of Worship, a collection of about thirty psalms and biblical songs in a variety of musical settings. It may be ordered from Materials Distribution Service, 341 Ponce de Leon Avenue, NE, Atlanta, GA 30365, or a Cokesbury Service Center.

Gradual Psalms (Church Hymnal Series VI) (The Church Hymnal Corporation, 1980, 1981, 1982). A three-volume collection of Gregorian psalm tones. Order from The Church Hymnal Corporation, 800 Second Avenue, New York, NY 10017.

	HL	HB	WB
Psalm 8			
Metrical version: O Lord, Our Lord, in All the Earth	—	95	515
(Alternate tune: St. Bernard)			
Gelineau: *The Gelineau Gradual,* p. 141			

Psalm 33
Gelineau: *The Gelineau Gradual,* pp. 39, 52, 105
Gregorian psalm tone: *Gradual Psalms,* Year C,
   Proper 14

Psalm 67			
Metrical version: Lord, Bless and Pity Us	—	493	456
Metrical version: God of Mercy, God of Grace.			
A Psalm Sampler			

	HL	HB	WB
Psalm 95			
Metrical version: O Come and Sing Unto the Lord	—	29	488
Metrical version: Come, Sing with Joy to God. *A Psalm Sampler*			
Through-composed: *A Psalm Sampler*			
Psalm 100			
Metrical version: All People That on Earth Do Dwell	1	25	288
Metrical version: Rejoice in God, All Earthly Lands. *A Psalm Sampler*			
Psalm 103			
Metrical: O Thou My Soul, Bless God the Lord	16	121	—
Paraphrase: O My Soul, Bless God, the Father	—	—	523
Gelineau: My Soul, Give Thanks to the Lord. *The Gelineau Gradual*, p. 77			
Psalm 117			
Metrical: From All That Dwell Below the Skies	388	33	373
Taizé: Laudate Dominum (Praise the Lord, All You Peoples). *Music from Taizé* (vocal edition), p. 10			
Psalm 121			
Metrical version: I to the Hills Will Lift My Eyes	—	377	430
Metrical version: I Looked, I Searched the Hills for Help. *A Psalm Sampler*			
Gelineau: I Lift Up My Eyes to the Mountains. *The Gelineau Gradual*, p. 127			
Psalm 136:1–9			
Metrical version: Let Us with a Gladsome Mind	64	28	453
Gelineau: O Give Thanks to the Lord. *The Gelineau Gradual*, pp. 147–150			
Psalm 145			
Metrical version: O Lord, You Are Our God and King	—	5	517
Gregorian psalm tone: *Gradual Psalms*, Year A, Proper 9			
Psalm 148			
Metrical version: Praise the Lord! Ye Heavens, Adore Him	10	3	554
(Alternate tune: Hyfrydol)			
Metrical version: Praise Ye, Praise Ye the Lord	—	98	—

Psalm 150 HL HB WB

Metrical version: Praise the Lord! God's Glories
  Show. *A Psalm Sampler*
Responsorial: Praise God in the Earthly Temple.
  A Psalm Sampler
Gregorian psalm tone: *Gradual Psalms,* Year A,
  Trinity Sunday

F. Selected Vocal Repertoire Appropriate to the Marriage Rite

The text of solos used in weddings should be God-centered, emphasizing the relationship between God and the church.

Bach, J. S.
  May God Smile on You. Duet (Peters) [M]
  My Heart Ever Faithful (G. Schirmer) [D]
  Wedding Prayer (Flammer) [M]
Brahms, Johannes
  Though I Speak with the Tongues *(Four Serious Songs)* (G. Schirmer)
  [D]
Busarow, Donald
  O Perfect Love (Concordia) [M]
  Lord, Who at Cana's Wedding Feast (Concordia) [M]
Fetler, Paul
  Wedding Song (Concordia) [M]
Gieseke, Richard W.
  Wedding Song (Concordia) [M]
Handel, G. F.
  Wedding Hymn (BMI Canada Ltd) [M]
Head, Michael
  Beloved, Let Us Love One Another (Boosey and Hawkes) [M]
Hopson, Hal H.
  The Gift of Love (Agape) [M]
Lovelace, Austin
  A Wedding Benediction (G. Schirmer) [M]
Mendelssohn, Felix
  Wedding Hymn (John Church Co.) [M]
Moe, Daniel
  The Greatest of These Is Love (Augsburg) [M]

Pelz, Walter
  A Wedding Blessing (Augsburg) [M]
Pinkham, Daniel
  A Wedding Song (Peters) [M]
  Wedding Cantata (Peters) [M]
Powell, Robert
  O Give Thanks (Sacred Music Press) [M]
  Walk in Love (Concordia) [M]
Proulx, Richard
  Nuptial Blessing (Augsburg) [M]
Schütz, Heinrich
  Wedding Song (Chantry Press) [ME]
Wetzler, Robert
  A Wedding Song (Augsburg) [M]
Willan, Healey
  Eternal Love (Harris) [M]
Williams, David H.
  A Wedding Prayer (H. W. Gray) [M]

Collections
A Ring of Gold, Seven Wedding Hymns, Donald Busarow (Concordia)
  [M]
Biblical Songs, Vols. 1 and 2, Antonín Dvořák (N. Simrock, Associated
  Music) [E to MD]
Cycle of Holy Songs, Ned Rorem (Southern Music)
Five Mystical Songs, Ralph Vaughan Williams (Galaxy)
Five Sacred Songs, Heinrich Schütz (Concordia) [M]
Five Wedding Songs, ed. Dale Wood (AMSI)
New Testament Songs, Sharon E. Rogers; Don McAfee; Bob Burroughs
  (Hope) [M]
Three Wedding Solos, G. Winston Cassler (Augsburg) [M]
Three Wedding Songs, Robert Powell (Concordia)
Seven Wedding Songs (Concordia)
Wedding Blessings, ed. Paul Bunjes (Concordia)

SOURCES OF THE LITURGICAL TEXTS

ASB *The Alternative Service Book 1980*. Church of England, 1980.
BCO *The Book of Common Order (1979)*. Church of Scotland, 1979.
BCP *The Book of Common Prayer*. Episcopal Church, U.S.A., 1977.
BCW *The Book of Common Worship*. Presbyterian, U.S.A., 1946.
CBW *The Covenant Book of Worship*. Evangelical Covenant Church of America, 1981.
LBW *Lutheran Book of Worship*. Lutheran, U.S.A., 1978.
SLD *The Service for the Lord's Day* (Supplemental Liturgical Resource 1). Presbyterian, U.S.A., 1984.
UCA *Uniting Church Worship Services: Marriage*. The Uniting Church in Australia, 1982.
UCC *Proposed Services of Marriage*. United Church of Christ, U.S.A., 1982.
WBK *The Worshipbook—Services and Hymns*. Presbyterian, U.S.A., 1972.

Abbreviations for Bible translations are:

NEB *The New English Bible*
PHI *The New Testament in Modern English*, J. B. Phillips
RSV *Revised Standard Version*
TEV *Today's English Version (Good News Bible)*

All Scripture quotations are from the RSV except as noted. The following quotations are altered: Num. 6:24–26 (pp. 22, 46, 50, 60) based on TEV as well as RSV; Ps. 37:3–4 (p. 61); Ps. 106:1 (p. 61); Ps. 118:24 (pp. 12, 25, 52); Jer. 31:33–34 (p. 26); Col. 3:12–14 (pp. 22, 38, 59) based on KJV as well as RSV; Col. 3:17 (pp. 22, 38, 59); 1 John 4:7–8 (p. 26); 1 John 4:16 (pp. 12, 25, 52).

The following Scripture quotations are from PHI: Rom. 8:34 (p. 27); and 2 Cor. 5:17 (p. 27), altered.

Ps. 95:1–2 (p. 61) is based on the RSV, TEV, and NEB.

Sources of liturgical texts are acknowledged as follows:

p. 12—"We have gathered . . ." was written for this resource, using elements borrowed from the BCO, BCP, and ASB.

p. 29—"_____ and _____ have come . . ." was written for this resource using elements borrowed from the BCO, BCP, and ASB.

pp. 13, 30, 54—"Gracious God, you are . . ." was written for this resource incorporating phrases from prayers in UCC and BCP.

pp. 15, 28, 55—"God of mercy, you have . . ." SLD, adapted.

pp. 16, 32—"I, _____, take you, _____, to be . . ." From BCW and other English-language liturgies, adapted.

pp. 18, 34—"This ring I give you . . ." BCW, adapted.

pp. 18, 34, 57—"Eternal God, creator . . ." BCP, adapted.

pp. 20, 36, 58—"Eternal God, without your grace . . ." WBK and CBW, adapted.

pp. 21, 37, 43, 49, 59—"Our Father in heaven . . ." is an agreed ecumenical text prepared by the International Consultation on English Texts.

pp. 21, 37, 59—"Those whom . . ." Based on RSV, NEB text of Mark 10:9.

p. 26—"Merciful God, we confess . . ." BCW, SLD, using BCP revision.

p. 27—"Almighty God, you created . . ." WBK, adapted.

p. 27—"Hear the good news! . . ." WBK, SLD, altered. Rom. 8:34 is from PHI. 2 Cor. 5:17 is based on a variant reading noted in the NEB.

p. 38—"O gracious God . . ." BCP, adapted.

pp. 40–42—The Great Prayer of Thanksgiving. The opening dialogue (pp. 40, 47) is an agreed ecumenical text prepared by the International Consultation on English Texts, with one slight alteration. In the last line the Consultation's text reads: "give him thanks." The text in this resource reads: "give our thanks." The "Holy, holy, holy Lord . . ." (p. 41) is an agreed ecumenical text prepared by the International Consultation on English Texts. The acclamation "Christ has died . . ." (p. 42) is from the sacramentary of the Roman Catholic Church (1974).

p. 44—"Because there is . . ." Based on NEB text of 1 Cor. 10:16–17.

p. 44—"The Lord Jesus, on the night . . ." Based on the RSV text of 1 Cor. 11:23–26, and Luke 22:19–20.

p. 45—"Loving God . . ." combines elements of prayers for use after Communion from SLD which were from *An Australian Prayer Book*, The Church of England in Australia, 1987; and *Uniting Church Worship Services: Holy Communion*, The Uniting Church in Australia, 1980.

pp. 46, 50—"Go out into the world . . ." WBK, SLD, altered. From proposed BCP of 1928.

p. 49—"Almighty and merciful God . . ." SLD, BCW (1906, 1932, 1946), revised.

p. 52—"_____ and _____ are married . . ." was written for this resource using elements borrowed from the BCO, BCP, and ASB.

p. 56—"_____, you are my wife, and I promise . . ." is adapted from BCW and other English-language liturgies.

p. 61—"Unless the Lord builds the house . . ." BCO, altered.

p. 63—"O God, you have made . . ." UCA.

p. 63—"Let us bless God . . ." LBW, altered.

p. 65—"Almighty God, giver of life . . ." ASB.

p. 65—"Almighty God, you have created . . ." ASB, altered.

p. 65—"Eternal God, in holy marriage . . ." ASB, altered.

FOR FURTHER READING

Bromiley, Geoffrey W. *God and Marriage.* Wm. B. Eerdmans Publishing Co., 1980.
 A theological statement on marriage which relates to God the creator, God the Son, and God the Holy Spirit.

Davies, J. G., ed. *The Westminster Dictionary of Worship.* Westminster Press, 1979.
 The entry entitled "Matrimony" (pp. 256–269) gives a concise liturgical history of the marriage rite in the early church and the various traditions that developed in both the East and the West.

Haughton, Rosemary. *The Theology of Marriage.* Butler, Wis.: Clergy Book Service, 1971.
 An excellent and concise treatment on the theology of Christian marriage by a Roman Catholic writer. The discussion considers the biblical foundations, how marriage came to be understood as a sacrament, and some common misconceptions about Christian marriage.

Liturgy, Journal of the Liturgical Conference, vol. 4, no. 2 (Spring 1984).
 A valuable collection of essays concerning the history and theology of Christmas marriage. Of special interest are the articles on the pastoral dimensions of marriage, appropriate biblical texts, and the sociological and anthropological dimensions of Christian marriage.

The Marriage Service with Music. Croydon, England: Royal School of Church Music.
 This collection contains hymns appropriate for wedding services.

Meyendorff, John. *Marriage: An Orthodox Perspective.* 2nd enl. ed. St. Vladimir's Seminary Press, 1975.
 This book is a fine presentation of Eastern Orthodox understandings of the meaning of Christian marriage and how it is celebrated. Included in

the text is a discussion about the use of crowning in the Orthodox wedding rite, the relationship of marriage and the Lord's Supper, and contemporary ethical issues concerning marriage.

Reformed Liturgy and Music.
A quarterly journal of the Office of Worship, on worship and music from the perspective of the Reformed tradition. It regularly includes articles on a variety of subjects by leaders in the field of worship. Regular columns, book reviews, and music reviews keep readers informed about resources and events and provide guidance to pastors, musicians, and worship committees. The journal regularly provides information about the development of the series of supplemental liturgical resources, of which this volume is the third. Articles on the subject of each supplemental resource are planned in relation to the publication of each resource.

————, vol. 20, no. 3 (Summer 1986).
This special issue of *Reformed Liturgy and Music* has Christian marriage as its theme and will be particularly useful in relation to the present volume, *Christian Marriage.* It includes practical articles on planning and leading the wedding. Copies may be secured from the Office of Worship, 1044 Alta Vista Road, Louisville, KY 40205. (Available August 1986.)

Schillebeeckx, Edward. *Marriage.* 2 vols. Sheed & Ward, 1965.
An important comprehensive treatment by a Roman Catholic scholar.

Stevenson, Kenneth. *Nuptial Blessing: A Study of Christian Marriage Rites.* Oxford University Press, 1983.
A recent and most comprehensive treatment available on the history and development of Christian marriage rites, including contemporary practices. Chapter 4, entitled "Reformulations," is an excellent treatment of the changes that occurred in the wedding rites at the time of the Reformation.

Von Allmen, Jean-Jacques. "The Celebration of Christian Marriage." In *Liturgical Review,* vol. 1, no. 1 (May 1978), pp. 1–17.
A high Reformed understanding of Christian marriage which calls for stricter standards in performing weddings. Von Allmen addresses the relationship between civil functions and ecclesiastical consecration, sacramental concerns, and the specifically Christian character of weddings.

White, James F. *Introduction to Christian Worship.* Abingdon Press, 1980.
Chapter 8, entitled "Passages," gives a helpful introduction to the liturgical, theological, and practical considerations surrounding the wedding service.

Willimon, William H. *The Service of God: Christian Worship and Work.* Abingdon Press, 1983.
Willimon focuses on two important ethical issues surrounding Christian marriage: the meaning of promises and the issue of procreation and the nurture of children.

————. *Worship as Pastoral Care*. Abingdon Press, 1979.
Chapter 6, entitled "Liturgy and Learning: The Wedding," argues that the marriage rite itself contains within it the material necessary and helpful for premarital counseling, catechesis for couple and congregation, and role change.

ACKNOWLEDGMENTS

Material from the following sources is acknowledged and is used by permission. Adaptations are by permission of copyright holders.

Scripture quotations from the *Revised Standard Version of the Bible* are copyrighted 1946, 1952, © 1971, 1973 by the Division of Christian Education of the National Council of the Churches of Christ in the U.S.A.

The Scripture quotation from *The New English Bible* is copyright © The Delegates of the Oxford University Press and The Syndics of the Cambridge University Press 1961, 1970.

The Scripture quotation from *The Good News Bible: The Bible in Today's English Version* is copyright © American Bible Society, 1976.

The Scripture quotation from *The New Testament in Modern English*, translated by J. B. Phillips, revised edition, is copyright © J. B. Phillips, 1958, 1959, 1966, 1972. Used by permission of Macmillan Publishing Company, Inc.

The preface dialogue to the great prayer of thanksgiving (pp. 40, 47); "Holy, holy, holy Lord" (p. 41); and the Lord's Prayer (pp. 21, 37, 43, 49, 59) are from *Prayers We Have in Common*, copyright © 1970, 1971, and 1975 by International Consultation on English Texts.

The Book of Common Worship, copyright © 1932 and 1946 by The Board of Christian Education of the Presbyterian Church in the United States of America. Used by permission of The Westminster Press.